Freshwater

Environmental Issues, Global Perspectives

Freshwater

James Fargo Balliett

SHARPE REFERENCE

an imprint of M.E. Sharpe, Inc.

SHARPE REFERENCE

Sharpe Reference is an imprint of M.E. Sharpe, Inc.

M.E. Sharpe, Inc.
80 Business Park Drive
Armonk, NY 10504

Library of Congress Cataloging-in-Publication Data

Balliett, James Fargo.
Freshwater: environmental issues, global perspectives / James Fargo Balliett.
    p. cm.
Includes bibliographical references and index.
ISBN 978-0-7656-8230-7 (hardcover: alk. paper)
1. Fresh water—Environmental aspects. 2. Water-supply—Environmental aspects. I. Title.

TD345.B345 2010
363.6'1—dc22   2010012122

Figures on pages 12, 38, and 52 by FoxBytes.

Printed and bound in the United States of America

The paper used in this publication meets the minimum requirements of
American National Standard for Information Sciences
Permanence of Paper for Printed Library Materials,
ANSI Z 39.48.1984.

(c) 10 9 8 7 6 5 4 3 2 1

Publisher: Myron E. Sharpe
Vice President and Director of New Product Development: Donna Sanzone
Vice President and Production Director: Carmen Chetti
Executive Development Editor: Jeff Hacker
Project Manager: Laura Brengelman
Program Coordinator: Cathleen Prisco
Assistant Editor: Alison Morretta
Text Design: Patrice Sheridan
Cover Design: Jesse Sanchez

Contents

Over the past 150 years, the planet Earth has undergone considerable environmental change, mainly as a result of the increasing number of people living on it. Unprecedented population growth has led to extensive development and natural resource consumption. A population that numbered 978 million people worldwide in 1800 reached 6.7 billion in 2009 and, according to the United Nations, may well exceed 8 billion by 2028.

This sixfold growth in population has brought about both positive and negative outcomes. Developments in medicine, various natural and social sciences, and advanced technology have resulted in widespread societal improvements. One measure of this success, average life expectancy, has climbed substantially. In the United States, life expectancy was 39.4 years in 1850; by 2009, it had grown to 77.9 years.

Another major change for global nations and cultures has been the accessibility and sharing of information. Though once isolated by oceans and geography, few communities remain untouched by technological innovation. The construction of jumbo jet planes, the development of advanced satellites and computers, and the power of the Internet have made travel and information readily available to an unprecedented number of people.

Technological advances have allowed residents of just about anywhere on the planet to share events and information almost instantly. For example, images of an expedition on the summit of Mount Everest or a scientific investigation in the middle of the Atlantic Ocean can be posted online via satellite and viewed by billions of citizens worldwide. In addition, cumulative and individual environmental impacts now can be assessed faster and more comprehensively than in years past.

During the same period, however, regulated and unregulated residential and business development that consumes natural resources has had profound impacts on the global environment. Such impacts are evident in the clear-cutting or burning of forests, whether this deforestation is for fuel or building materials, or simply to clear the land for other activities; the drainage of wetlands to divert freshwater, expand agriculture, or provide more building upland; the overfishing of oceans to meet an ever-growing appetite for seafood; the stripping of mountaintops for fuel, metals, or minerals; and the pollution of freshwater sources by the waste output of industrial and residential communities. In fact, pollution has spread across land, air, and water biomes in ever-increasing concentrations, causing considerable damage, especially to fragile ecosystems.

The Emergence of a Global Perspective

Environmental Issues, Global Perspectives provides a fresh look at critical environmental issues from an international viewpoint. The series consists of five individual volumes: *Wetlands, Forests, Mountains, Oceans,* and *Freshwater.* Relying on the latest accepted principles of science—the acquisition of knowledge based on reasoning, experience, and experiments—each volume presents information and analysis in a clear, objective manner. The overarching goal of the series is to explore how human population growth and behavior have changed the world's natural areas, especially in negative ways, and how modern society has responded to the challenges these changes present—often through increased educational efforts, better conservation, and management of the environment.

Each book is divided into three parts. The first part provides background information on the biome being discussed: how such ecosystems are formed, the relative size and locations of such areas, key animal and plant species that tend to live in such environments, and how the health of each biome affects our planet's environment as a whole. All five titles present the most recent scientific data on the topic and also examine how humans have relied on each biome for survival and stability, including food, water, fuel, and economic growth.

The second part of each book contains in-depth chapters examining seven different geographically diverse locations. An overview of each area details its unique features, including geology, weather conditions, and endemic species. The text also examines the health of the natural environment and discusses the local human population. Short- and long-term environmental impacts are assessed, and regional and international efforts to address interrelated social, economic, and environmental issues are presented in detail.

The third part of each book studies how the cumulative levels of pollution and aggressive resource consumption affect each biome on a global scale. It provides readers with examples of local and regional impacts—filled-in wetlands, decimated forests, overdeveloped mountainsides, empty fishing grounds, and polluted freshwater—as well as responses to these problems. Although each book's conclusion is different, scenarios are highlighted that present collective efforts to address environmental issues. Sometimes, these unique efforts have resulted in a balance between resource conservation and consumption.

The *Environmental Issues, Global Perspectives* series reveals that—despite the distance of geography in each title's case studies—a common set of human-induced ecological pressures and challenges turns up repeatedly. In some areas, evidence of improved resource management or reduced environmental impacts is positive, with local or national cooperation and the application of new technology providing measurable results. In other areas, however, weak laws or unenforced regulations have allowed environmental damage to continue unchecked: Brazen frontiersmen continue to log remote rain forests, massive fishing trawlers still use mile-long nets to fill their floating freezers in the open ocean, and communities, businesses, vehicles, factories, and power plants continue to pollute the air, land, and water resources. Such existing problems and emerging issues, such as global climate change, threaten not just specific animal and plant communities, but also the health and well-being of the very world we live in.

Wetlands

Wetlands encompass a diversity of habitats that rely on the presence of water to survive. Over the last two centuries, these hard-to-reach areas have been viewed with disdain or eliminated by a public that saw them only as dangerous and worthless lowlands. The *Wetlands* title in this series tracks changing perceptions of one of the world's richest and biologically productive biomes and efforts that have been undertaken to protect many areas. With upland and coastal development resulting in the loss of more than half of the world's wetlands, significant efforts now are under way to protect the 5 million square miles (13 million square kilometers) of wetlands that remain.

In *Wetlands*, three noteworthy examples demonstrate the resilience of wetland plants and animals and their ability to rebound from human-induced pressures: In Central Asia, the Aral Sea and its adjacent wetlands show promising regrowth, in part because of massive hydrology projects being implemented to undo years of damage to the area. The Everglades wetlands complex, spanning the lower third of Florida, is slowly reviving as restorative conservation measures are implemented. And Lake Poyang in southeastern China has experienced increased ecological health as a result of better resource management and community education programs focused on the vital role that wetlands play in a healthy environment.

Forests

Forests are considered the lungs of the planet, as they consume and store carbon dioxide and produce oxygen. These biomes, defined as ecological communities dominated by long-lived woody vegetation, historically have provided an economic foundation for growing nations, supplying food for both local and distant markets, wood for buildings, firewood for fuel, and land for expanding cities and farms. For centuries, industrial nations such as Great Britain, Italy, and the United States have relied on large tracts of forestland for economic prosperity.

The research presented in the *Forests* title of this series reveals that population pressures are causing considerable environmental distress in even the most remote forest areas. Case studies provide an assessment of illegal logging deep in South America's Amazon Rain Forest, a region closely tied to food and product demands thousands of miles away; an examination of the effect of increased hunting in Central Africa's Congo forest, which threatens wildlife, especially mammal species with slower reproductive cycles; and a profile of encroachment on old-growth tropical forests on the Southern Pacific island of Borneo, which today is better managed, thanks to the collective planning and conservation efforts of the governments of Brunei, Indonesia, and Malaysia.

Mountains

Always awe-inspiring, mountainous areas contain hundreds of millions of years of history, stretching back to the earliest continental landforms. Mountains are characterized by their distinctive geological, ecological, and biological conditions. Often, they are so large that they create their own weather patterns. They also store nearly one-third of the world's freshwater—in the form of ice and snow—on their slopes. Despite their daunting size and often formidable climates, mountains are affected by growing local populations, as well as by distant influences, such as air pollution and global climate change.

The case studies in the *Mountains* book consider how global warming in East Africa is harming Mount Kenya's regional population, which relies on mountain runoff to irrigate farms for subsistence crops; examine the fragile ecology of the South Island mountains in New Zealand's Southern Alps and consider how development threatens the region's endemic plant and animal species; and discuss the impact of mountain use over time in New Hampshire's White Mountains, where stricter management efforts have been used to limit the growing footprint of millions of annual visitors and alpine trekkers.

Oceans

Covering 71 percent of the planet, these saline bodies of water likely provided the unique conditions necessary for the building blocks of life to form billions of years ago. Today, our oceans continue to support life in important ways: by providing the largest global source of protein in the form of fish populations, by creating and influencing weather systems, and by absorbing waste streams, such as airborne carbon.

Oceans have an almost magnetic draw—almost half of the world's population lives within a few hours of an ocean. Although oceans are vast in size, exceeding 328 million cubic miles (1.37 billion cubic kilometers), they have been influenced by and have influenced humans in numerous ways.

The case studies in the *Oceans* title of this series focus on the most remote locations along the Mid-Atlantic Ridge, where new ocean floor is being formed 20,000 feet (6,100 meters) underwater; the Maldives, a string of islands in the Indian Ocean, where increasing sea levels may force residents to abandon some communities by 2020; and the North Sea at the edge of the Arctic Ocean, where fishing stocks have been dangerously depleted as a result of multiple nations' unrelenting removal of the smallest and largest species.

Freshwater

Freshwater is our planet's most precious resource, and it also is the least conserved. Freshwater makes up only 3 percent of the total water on the planet, and yet the majority (1.9 percent) is held in a frozen state in glaciers, icebergs, and polar ice fields. This leaves only 1.1 percent of the total volume of water on the planet as freshwater available in liquid form.

The final book in this series, *Freshwater*, tracks the complex history of the steady growth of humankind's water consumption, which today reaches some 3.57 quadrillion gallons (13.5 quadrillion liters) per year. Along with a larger population has come the need for more drinking water, larger farms requiring greater volumes of water for extensive irrigation, and more freshwater to support business and industry. At the same time, such developments have led to lowered water supplies and increased water pollution.

The case studies in *Freshwater* look at massive water systems such as that of New York City and the efforts required to transport this freshwater and protect these resources; examine how growth has affected freshwater quality in the ecologically unique and geographically isolated Lake Baikal region of eastern Russia; and study the success story of the privatized freshwater system in Chile and consider how that country's water sources are threatened by climate change.

Acknowledgments

I owe the greatest debt to my wonderful Mom and Dad, Nancy and Whitney, who led me to the natural world as a child. Thank you for encouraging curiosity and creativity, and for teaching me to be strong in the midst of a storm. I also could not have gotten this far without steady support, expert advice, and humorous optimism from my siblings: Blue, Julie, Will, and Whit.

I greatly appreciate the input of Dr. Arri Eisen, Director of the Program in Science and Society at Emory University, at key stages of this project. My sincere thanks also go to the superb team at M.E. Sharpe, including Donna Sanzone, Cathy Prisco, and Laura Brengelman, as well as Gina Misiroglu, Jennifer Acker, Deborah Ring, Patrice Sheridan, and Leslee Anderson. Any title that explores science and the environment faces daunting hurdles of ever-changing data and a need for the highest accuracy. This series benefited greatly from their precise work and steady guidance.

Finally, *Environmental Issues, Global Perspectives* would not have been possible without the efforts of the many scientists, researchers, policy experts, regulators, conservationists, and writers with a vested interest in the environment.

The last few decades of the twentieth century brought a significant change in awareness and attitudes toward the health of this planet. Scholars and laypeople alike shifted their view of the environment from something simply to be consumed and conquered now to a viewpoint of it as a significant asset because of its capacities for such measurable benefits as flood control, water filtration, oxygen creation, pollution storage and processing, and biodiversity support, as well as other positive features.

Knowledge of Earth's finiteness and vulnerability has resulted in substantially better stewardship. My thanks go to those people who, through their visions and hard work, have taught the next generation that fundamental science is essential and that humankind's collective health is inextricably tied to the global environment.

James Fargo Balliett
Cape Cod, Massachusetts

INTRODUCTION
TO FRESHWATER

1 The Wonders of Freshwater

Water is a paramount resource on planet Earth. Four billion years ago, it played a central role in the creation and evolution of living creatures, which continue to rely on it as a vital, life-sustaining resource. Although the planet was named nearly 1,000 years ago after the Anglo-Saxon word *erda,* meaning "soil," a more apt name might have been *oceanus,* meaning "ocean," due to the abundance of water.

Of the world's 328 million cubic miles (1,367 million cubic kilometers) of water, salt water from the oceans makes up 96.5 percent of the total. The remaining 3.5 percent consists of freshwater, the majority of which (1.74 percent of all water) is frozen in the polar ice caps and glaciers; 1.7 percent, a fraction of the worldwide water total, is available to humankind on or below the surface in freshwater liquid form such as ponds, lakes, streams, rivers, wetlands, and underground aquifers.

Of the 1.75 million species that have been identified worldwide living in both terrestrial and marine environments, some 80 percent rely on freshwater to survive, as their bodies cannot process salt water. In fact, ingestion of salt water by humans can be deadly. Human kidneys, similar to the organs of other living creatures, can only remove a certain amount of salt (sodium chloride) from water before they begin to draw freshwater from other cellular tissue to compensate. If too much salt water is consumed, a chain reaction results in kidney failure, as well as the loss of nerve and muscle functions, eventually causing death by heart failure or seizure. The fact that so much life on the planet relies on freshwater, a resource that makes up such a small percentage of the total, is an incredible scenario.

ASSESSMENT OF GLOBAL WATER SOURCES

Location (Type)	Amount of Time Held	Percentage of Worldwide Total
Oceans/seas (salt water)	Thousands of years	97.4
Polar ice caps/ice floes, glaciers (freshwater)	Thousands of years	1.9
Groundwater (freshwater in bedrock)	Days to thousands of years	0.6
Soils and permafrost (freshwater)	Days to weeks	0.0809
Lakes (freshwater)	Days to years	0.008
Atmosphere (freshwater)	Days to weeks	0.001
Rivers (freshwater)	Days to weeks	0.0001

Source: United Nations Educational, Scientific, and Cultural Organization. *U.N. World Water Development Report: Water in a Changing World.* London, United Kingdom, 2009.

Freshwater Defined

Water is a dynamic substance. It is a chemical compound made from three atoms: two hydrogen and one oxygen. Under a microscope, the molecules look somewhat like a mouse's head, with two smaller hydrogen atoms attached on opposite sides (105-degree angles) to the larger oxygen atom. The two hydrogen atoms are positively charged, while the oxygen atom is negatively charged, and this draws the two elements together.

Water on Earth has several universal properties. It is the only known substance that can exist in three states of matter simultaneously—that is, in a liquid, solid (frozen), or gaseous state. A critical medium for dissolved chemicals, it is able to hold more than seventy elements at the same time.

In order for water to be classified as freshwater, it must contain less than .05 percent of dissolved salts. Ocean salt water typically has between 3.1 and 3.8 percent salinity.

Each molecule of water has two hydrogen nuclei, and these are held to a central oxygen molecule with two charged electrons. This very durable molecular structure, also called a covalent chemical bond, can absorb large amounts of energy with little change in temperature because of the way the hydrogen bonds are connected to the oxygen molecules. This structure also means that it is easy to adhere other chemicals to water; thus, water often is referred to as a "universal solvent."

Although scientists once thought that water was an individual element, it is, in fact, a compound substance, and water molecules readily change their structure as the temperature changes:

- When water turns into a gas (when heated to 212 degrees Fahrenheit, or 100 degrees Celsius), the vapor molecules are far apart from each other. In this phase, the molecules do not bond easily, because they are moving too quickly.

- When water becomes a liquid (between 211 degrees Fahrenheit, or 99 degrees Celsius, and 33 degrees Fahrenheit, or 1 degree Celsius), the individual molecules bond to each other but do not hold on tightly. The connections between droplets constantly change in form and size. As the temperature decreases, they grow tighter in formation.

- When water transforms into ice (when cooled below 32 degrees Fahrenheit/0 degrees Celsius), the bonds are altered to lock into a tight formation held together by hydrogen bonds. The solid connections give ice hardness and durability.

The History of Freshwater

Five billion years ago, the solar system was still developing. The sun was in the process of forming, and a massive amount of solid and gaseous material began to swirl around it in a cloud of debris. The considerable gravitational pull of the sun eventually pressed dust, rocks, and gases into clusters. These masses, also called proto-planetary discs, eventually took the shape of eight planets, five dwarf planets, dozens of smaller moons, and thousands of meteors and asteroids.

Over millions of years, these balls of matter took shape and established orbits a certain distance from a new sun. Earth eventually positioned itself roughly 93 million miles (150 million kilometers) from this sun. Approximately 4.5 billion years ago, the molten Earth began the slow process of cooling. Dense materials, such as nickel, flowed toward the center of the planet, and lighter materials, such as basalt, gravitated toward the outside.

Trapped deep inside the Earth's bedrock under intense pressure was a large amount of water. It slowly emerged on the surface as a liquid and gas through wide cracks or fissures in the surface of the bedrock or was released by the eruption of volcanoes. Over time, the lower-lying basins and valleys collected this water.

By 500 million years ago, a single, large body of water had formed. The estimated volume of this water was 343 sextillion (which is a number followed by

21 zeroes) gallons (1.3 sextillion liters), which is close to the volume of today's oceans combined. However, 96.5 percent of the planet-wide water eventually contained dissolved sodium, chlorine, magnesium, and calcium, turning it into a salty brew that was distinctly different from freshwater. The amount that did not contain these elements (a little more than 3.4 percent) could be found in three main places: in the atmosphere, such as in clouds and storms; underground, held in place by rocks; and at the surface, in rivers, streams, and polar ice.

The presence of so much water, both saline and fresh, also played a central role in the formation of the Earth's atmosphere and the evolution of land and water species. When the planet first formed, Earth's air was full of helium and sulfur, but eventually nitrogen and oxygen were the majority components of the air, similar to what is breathed in today. The chemical transformation of the atmosphere was primarily due to the presence, over millions of years, of oxygen-producing aquatic plants called algae.

The Hydrologic Cycle

Although today's oceans cover 71 percent of the planet, the distribution and volume of freshwater varies from place to place, depending on weather patterns. In addition, all unfrozen water is in constant motion. Moving from one area of the planet to another, water repeatedly circulates through a series of states commonly known as the hydrologic cycle.

Sometimes the pattern of water movement is predictable, but it also may be random. For example, rain falls on the Earth's surface, and this precipitation trick-

COMPARISON OF FRESHWATER AND SALT WATER CHEMICAL CONTENTS		
Element	Freshwater (Rainwater, ppm*)	Salt Water (Typical, ppm)
Calcium	0.2	412
Chloride	0.2	19,500
Magnesium	0.05	1,290
Potassium	0.1	380
Silicate	0	7
Sodium	0.2	10,770

*ppm=parts per million

Source: Trevor Day. Lakes and Rivers. New York: Chelsea House, 2006.

les above and below land to arrive in rivers. Once there, the water is transported to the oceans. Along the way, some water evaporates back into the atmosphere.

As water moves, air pressure and temperature variations cause its molecules to shrink, expand, accelerate, or slow down. Five main processes are included in the hydrologic cycle: 1) evaporation; 2) condensation; 3) transpiration; 4) percolation; and 5) precipitation.

Evaporation

Evaporation occurs when water in an ocean, lake, pond, puddle, or other body changes from a liquid to a gas after being heated by the sun or another energy source, such as underground magma. As water turns to a gas, the molecules speed up their molecular movement, eventually breaking apart from one another. The vapor that forms often is carried away to another location by thermal currents or wind.

Evaporation rates are controlled by a number of factors, including the type of water (fresh or salt), the surface area of the water, the movement of air over the water, the temperatures of the air and water, and the intensity of heat applied to the water. The number of salts present in ocean water makes its evaporation rate slower than that of freshwater. At any given time, the atmosphere contains roughly 3,094 cubic miles (12,900 cubic kilometers) of freshwater; some 90 percent of this content is from evaporation.

Condensation

The process of condensation is the reverse of evaporation. It occurs when cool air, or contact with a cooler substance, causes water vapor to form into droplets of liquid water.

When air flows above the land and a mountain forces the air upward to a higher elevation, the mixing of warm and cool air results in gaseous water. The end result is the formation of clouds and often rain droplets.

Another instance of condensation occurs when a glass is filled with cold water and ice cubes on a hot, humid day. When warm air around the glass comes in contact with the colder surface, droplets of water form on the outside of the glass. The dew that forms on the ground when cool night air comes into contact with rising warm water vapor also is caused by condensation.

Transpiration

Transpiration happens when water evaporates from the leaves, stems, and roots of plants. Approximately 10 percent of the water in the atmosphere is due to plant transpiration. This process occurs when plants and trees move water through their roots and vascular system. It also happens during the performance of photosynthesis. As vegetation takes in carbon dioxide and releases oxygen, the expenditure of energy is tremendous (combined, it is more than ten times the electric power used planet-wide in 2009). As part of the cooling process, a large amount of water evaporates from the vegetation's roots, stems, and leaves.

Transpiration for a full-grown tree may amount to several hundred gallons of freshwater on a summer day. In drier climates, trees such as conifers and plants such as cacti have adapted to release minimal water through a number of adaptations, including smaller physical dimensions, reduced leaf size, long periods of dormancy, and moisture-retaining bark.

Percolation

Percolation occurs when water soaks downward through the surface of the ground. This process, which also is called infiltration, occurs when water moves through rocks and soil to become groundwater. It may take hours or even years to complete.

As the water travels through cracks of bedrock and layers of sand and soils, gravity directs the percolation in a downward direction. Depending on the height of the water table, groundwater supplies may be near the surface or deeper in the ground. In more arid communities, the water table may be hundreds of feet below ground.

Precipitation

When a storm deposits rain or snow, the moisture that falls is called precipitation. This is the culmination of several distinct events.

First, condensation increases the size of tiny water droplets floating in the atmosphere. These larger molecules then cluster with others to form larger clouds containing more water. Once the droplets exceed the size of about 1 percent of an inch in length, clouds release the droplets from the sky as rain or, if it is colder, as sleet, snow, or hail.

Underground Freshwater

The great majority of available (not frozen in ice) freshwater (some 99 percent) sits underground and is held in place by layers of rock. Known as groundwater, nearly 5.6 million cubic miles (23.4 million cubic kilometers) of such water is stored up to 3 miles (4.8 kilometers) deep within the Earth. The total volume

The Groundwater Replenishment System in Fountain Valley, California, is the largest water treatment system of its kind in the world. It converts the sewage water of Orange County into drinking water, which is then returned to underground aquifers to boost stored water and to reduce the intrusion of salt water from the Pacific Ocean. Population growth, recurring droughts, and a decline in imported water supplies have led to water needs exceeding the county's freshwater supply. *(Mary Knox Merrill/Christian Science Monitor/Getty Images)*

of groundwater is nearly 114 times the volume of river water (509 cubic miles, or 2,122 cubic kilometers) and lake water (42,320 cubic miles, or 176,398 cubic kilometers) combined.

This subsurface water is typically fresh; exceptions include coastal areas, where salt water has crept into bedrock. In all cases, the water contains dissolved elements of the rocks surrounding it. Some water may include radioactive isotopes, naturally occurring in rock formations. Other water sources contain iron, manganese, and sulfur.

The underground environment is difficult to understand, because it cannot be seen from the surface. Using technology such as sonar waves, geologists have learned about the diverse ways in which water is held underground.

Groundwater is primarily replenished through rain and snowmelt. Sometimes, a large fracture in rock such as limestone or basalt fills with water. Over time, a small opening is widened by the dissolving action of water running across the rock surface. Eventually, a series of connected channels or caves may hold hundreds of millions of gallons of water. Underground freshwater pools held by nonporous rock and thick layers of sediment are called aquifers. The movement of freshwater in aquifers is directed by elevation changes and gravity.

Some underground locations host a large amount of water, and this causes great pressure, which, in turn, pushes water toward a surface location. This results in an artesian well, a phenomenon named after the French province Artois where residents have accessed freshwater from groundwater wells without using pumps for hundreds of years.

Groundwater flow feeds rivers and lakes. At the point where groundwater intersects with a stream or pond or another body of surface water, it flows directly into these water bodies. Some rivers rely on groundwater inflow for as much as 50 percent of their water content.

Groundwater is the most common source of public water supplies, especially where lakes and rivers are unavailable. Within an aquifer, the upper limit of water is called the water table. Depending on a number of variables, including the type of underground material, water volume, size of aquifer, and inflow of water, wells can withdraw a certain amount of water from below the water table to supply freshwater for use by individual homeowners, businesses, or to a town or city. At least one-quarter of all groundwater is extremely difficult to access due to its depth or position underground.

Aboveground Freshwater

The freshwater that is visible at the Earth's surface makes up only .013 percent of the total water sources and is made up of a number of different formations, including ponds, lakes, streams, rivers, and wetlands. These water bodies are fed through several sources, including groundwater, snowmelt, and rain.

This surface water is supported by bedrock or soils, like clay, that are not very porous. Without this support, the water would soak underground and become groundwater. Surface water, fed by all forms of precipitation (rain, snow, fog) as well as groundwater inflow, is noteworthy because it often is in steady motion, moving from one location to another due to geography and elevation changes.

Ponds and Lakes

The largest bodies of surface freshwater include ponds and lakes. These form through several, and sometimes combined, processes. When a glacier recedes across a landscape, it often leaves behind depressions in the land. A sinkhole created by flooding also can create such a feature. Similarly, an earthquake or large tectonic rift often creates large basins. And a river that changes its course to carve a new bend and then returns to its original path, called an oxbow, may leave behind a curved depression. Once the land is altered in this way, the hole fills up with water from one or more of the following sources: rainwater, groundwater, surface flow, or inflow from a river or another pond or lake.

Always unique in size, depth, and water characteristics, ponds and lakes around the world share one distinct feature: Most eventually will fill in with sediment and organic material and will become dry land. This process relies on the slow accumulation of dead plant and animal material within the bottom of a water body. It may take tens of thousands or several million years to occur, but, over time, the majority will transform from open water to a wetland to an upland biome such as a forest.

Ponds and lakes have varying water chemistry, due to different levels of sunlight exposure, upland runoff, water currents, air and water temperature, and animal and plant life. A eutrophic lake contains a high inflow of nitrogen and phosphorus to support rich plant life. A mesotrophic lake has average nutrient and oxygen levels in the water, supporting a moderate level of vegetation. An oligotrophic lake features the clearest water but also the fewest nutrients and resident species.

There are approximately 304 million freshwater ponds and lakes on the planet, covering more than 3 percent of the land area. Nine out of ten of these bodies of water are less than an acre in size. Some are just a dozen feet in diameter.

The largest freshwater body of water, the Capsian Sea (bordered by eastern Azerbaijan, northern Iran, southern Russia, and western Kazakhstan and Turmenistan), spans 270 miles (434 kilometers) across from east to west and is 750 miles (1,207 kilometers) long from north to south. Although named a sea due to its enormous size (149,200 square miles or 386,428 square kilometers), this 5.5-million-year-old freshwater lake is fed by 130 separate rivers. Because it has no outlet, the Caspian Sea has almost 1.2 percent salinity (roughly a third of the salinity of the Atlantic Ocean).

The difference in definition between a pond and a lake is size. Most ponds are less than an acre in size, and some may be only a few inches deep. Many ponds are spring fed by groundwater, whereas most lakes have a river inlet and outlet. In total, ponds and lakes around the world are estimated to contain 42,829 cubic miles (178,520 cubic kilometers) of freshwater.

The Great Lakes in North America (In order of size: Superior, Huron, Michigan, Erie, and Ontario) are so large that they often are referred to as freshwater inland seas. Spanning a total of 94,710 square miles (245,299 square kilometers), the Great Lakes' combined freshwater total is 5,438 cubic miles (22,667 cubic kilometers). If the water in these lakes was poured across the continental United States, the water would be 10 feet (3 meters) deep. When combined with Eastern Russia's Lake Baikal, these water bodies account for 40 percent of the Earth's surface freshwater.

Rivers and Streams

On a given day, all of the rivers on the planet hold only .0002 percent of Earth's total freshwater volume. Worldwide, there are 263 river basins. Twenty-eight of these contain major freshwater rivers that span multiple countries.

There are several types of flowing water bodies, which are defined mainly by the volume of water that flows through them. A river is the biggest flowing body. It has a permanent or seasonal flow that amounts to a large volume that drains in to a large lake or ocean body. A stream is a smaller, narrow body of water that often drains into a river. A brook, spring, or creek is the smallest flowing water body, and it often drains into a stream.

Most river basins are defined by their volume as well as length. The largest rivers are up to 4,000 miles (6,436 kilometers) long. Some of the basins have a geologic history that stretches back hundreds of millions of years. These rivers, streams, and small water bodies work like conveyer belts, carrying sediments, nutrients, and debris from locations at higher elevations to lower ones.

Although many watersheds span extensive upland areas, the rivers that drain through them do not carry very much in terms of total freshwater volume. For example, the Ob River, which stretches across western Russia, is 2,268 miles (3,649 kilometers) long. As the seventh-longest river in the world, it has 9,300 miles (14,964 kilometers) of navigable waterways. Its watershed is 1.1 million

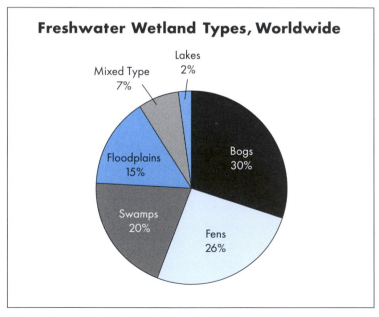

Source: Ramsar Covention, Wetlands Inventory, 2004.

square miles (2.8 million square kilometers) in size, and during springtime it discharges an average of 441,500 cubic feet (12,502 cubic meters) of water per second. However, where it empties into the Arctic Sea, it only releases 5.2 inches (13.2 centimeters) in annual average runoff, primarily due to atmospheric, human, plant, and animal consumption of the water along its path. If rain and snow over the entire watershed were to completely halt, the Ob River would run dry in one month.

Another large river, Egypt's Nile River spans a section of semi-arid desert and surpasses 4,000 miles (6,436 kilometers) in length. Yet the Nile has less than 0.5 inch (1.2 centimeters) of annual average runoff directly into the Mediterranean Sea, due to water removals and the hot and dry conditions along its route.

A stream, which is identified in the United States as a watercourse that is less than 60 feet (18 meters) wide, plays an important role in distributing surface water through a specific portion of a watershed. Most streams rely on precipitation and, particularly in warmer months with less rain, may be reduced to only a small flow, kept active by the infiltration of groundwater from adjacent topography.

Wetlands

Wetlands have a similar formation pattern to lakes and ponds. These biomes represent a transition zone between upland and deeper water habitats. They often form where there is not enough water to create a pond or lake but the land still is too wet to support traditional upland species like large trees.

Given this variability, scientists around the world have developed fifty different definitions for a wetland, because they occur in such diverse conditions. Three of the more common types of wetlands include swamps, such as forested, shrub, and mangrove; bogs, known for a layer of sponge-like vegetation on the surface; and marshes, which are located near larger bodies of water such as ponds, lakes, and rivers. There are approximately 4.9 million square miles (13 million square kilometers) of wetlands on Earth.

Due to their shallow depths, the combination of all wetlands on the planet only holds 2,752 cubic miles (11,471 cubic kilometers) of freshwater, which is just less than the amount held by the entire atmosphere. Historically, the general public and government agencies have undervalued wetlands as compared to other bodies of freshwater, deeming them as something to be avoided or eliminated due to the perception of a wetland as a host for diseases and as wasted real estate.

In fact, these areas provide considerable environmental services to a region. The plant material and microbiological residents filter water that moves through them, turning toxic waste that enters the wetland into nearly potable water upon exit. Wetlands support a diversity of plants and animals that rely on such ecosystems for food and shelter. Wetlands also serve as storm buffers to upland communities, absorbing large amounts of water in sudden rains or floods and releasing it slowly afterward.

Life Relies on Water

There are approximately 1.75 million identified terrestrial and aquatic species living on Earth—and this number may be as high as 30 million. Water plays a critical role in the lives of all plants and animals, and every living creature relies on some type of water to live. Mitochondrial deoxyribonucleic acid (DNA), the most basic cellular building block, is made of water, and most living things are made up of a large percentage of water.

Temperature Regulation

An everyday function of water includes temperature regulation. Because of its chemical construction of two hydrogen and one oxygen molecules, water is a dynamic and durable solvent. One demonstration of this can be seen in how freshwater resists rapid temperature changes, which helps animal and plant organisms live in a more stable environment. Water requires five times more heat energy than materials such as rock or exposed ground to elevate in temperature by 1 degree Fahrenheit (0.6 degrees Celsius). Large amounts of water, such as a deepwater lake, actually can cool the surrounding environment in warm periods, as well as keep the surrounding environment warmer during cool periods.

The water that organisims hold in their bodies functions the same way. Bodily water content plays a key role in thermoregulation, allowing a species to cool or heat itself without exerting additional energy.

Nutrients and Hydration

Water also is an impressive nutrient holder. The molecular construction of freshwater makes it an excellent medium to contain a spectrum of nutrients for both plants and animals. While nutrient levels vary from source to source, an average sample of freshwater may contain up to twenty-one minerals essential for biological metabolic existence. These include boron, calcium, chlorine, chromium, copper, fluorine, iron, magnesium, manganese, molybdenum, nickel, phosphorus, potassium, silicon, sodium, and zinc.

Scientific studies show that the mineral content in water supports bone and cell membrane health, hydration and electrolyte balance, metabolic functions, hormone functions, and neurological signal transmission. A 2005

World Health Organization review of eighty international studies, combining approximately fifty years of research, found a strong correlation between mineral-rich water ingestion and overall human health. More specifically, the studies revealed that low incidences of cardiovascular problems were linked to drinking sufficient quantities of mineral-rich water.

Plant Cell Structure

Water plays a central role in the cell structure of vegetation as well. Plants have evolved efficient mechanisms to acquire, store, and release freshwater.

The leaves of a plant have very small depressions called pores, or stomata. Often found on the underside of a leaf, they are able to open and close to allow or limit the loss of water during photosynthesis.

Plant and tree roots also contain a unique structure for water management. When water is needed, a main root body uses its tens of thousands of tiny root hairs (each 3/1,000 of an inch thick) to absorb freshwater through cellular channels. Some trees may hold more than 26,000 gallons (98,421 liters) of water at one time in order to stay adequately hydrated during a dry period.

Selected Web Sites

American Water Works Association: http://www.awwa.org.

European Union Water Site: http://ec.europa.eu/environment/water/index_en. htm.

Hydrologic Cycle, Michigan State University: http://www.iwr.msu.edu/edmodule/ water/cycle.htm.

Nutrients in Drinking Water, World Health Organization: http://www.who.int/ water_sanitation_health/dwq/nutrientsindw/en/index.html.

Public Water Supply and Use, U.S. Geological Survey: http://ga.water.usgs.gov/ edu/wups.html.

United Nations World Water Development Report: http://www.unesco.org/water/ wwap/wwdr/wwdr1/table_contents/index.shtml.

Further Reading

Benjamin, Mark. *Water Chemistry*. New York: McGraw-Hill, 2001.

Boyd, Claude E. *Water Quality: An Introduction*. Norwell, MA: Kluwer Academic, 2000.

Brutsaert, Wilfried. *Hydrology: An Introduction*. New York: Cambridge University Press, 2005.

Cech, Thomas V. *Principles of Water Resources: History, Development, Management and Policy.* Hoboken, NJ: John Wiley and Sons, 2009.

Gleick, Peter H., et al. *The World's Water 2008–2009: The Biennial Report on Freshwater Resources.* Washington, DC: Island, 2008.

Moss, Brian. *Ecology of Fresh Waters: Man and Medium.* Malden, MA: Blackwell Science, 2010.

United Nations. *Water: A Shared Responsibility.* Washington, DC: United Nations Environment Programme, 2006.

2 | Humans and Freshwater

Humans cannot survive without freshwater. The average adult male body is 65 percent water; the adult female body is 58 percent water; and a newborn baby's is 77 percent water. Different parts of the body have varying water levels. Bones contain 22 percent water, fat has approximately 25 percent, muscle contains up to 76 percent, and blood contains 83 percent. The human brain is made of 74 percent water.

How much freshwater an individual requires for hydration is based on his or her environment, physical activity, size, and overall health. Nutritionists recommend that an average person drink between 9 and 14 cups of water per day to stay hydrated; strenuous activity requires up to double that amount.

While humans can survive without food for a few weeks, they cannot survive without water. Once the body is deprived of all water, irreversible damage can occur to internal organs, such as the kidneys, liver, and heart, and can lead to death.

Water plays a vital role inside the human body. It delivers critical oxygen, as well as essential nutrients such as calcium, iron, magnesium, potassium, and sodium. It serves as a medium for transporting proteins, carbohydrates, and fats, as well as removing waste products. It is used as the primary solvent for the creation of blood, mucous, spinal fluid, sweat, tears, and other bodily fluids. It helps with the digestion and absorption of nutrients from foods. And it helps maintain the temperature of the human body.

A human being's central nervous system relies on water to transport hundreds of millions of neurological signals per day. The circulatory system uses water to form and replenish tissue to support the heart valves. The brain and spinal cord sit in a protective bath of nutrients and mostly water. And the skeleton uses water to create and maintain strong bones and as a lubricant between joints.

After spending up to two weeks inside the human body, the average droplet of water is expelled, often along with unwanted toxins and wastes. An adult human discharges up to 2 quarts (1.8 liters) of water through urine and feces each day, up to a pint (0.5 liter) of water through breathing, and about a pint (0.5 liter) through perspiration, depending on a person's activity level.

Human Advancements and Water

Throughout history, the availability of freshwater has been instrumental in the major advancements of civilizations. Abundant sources of water have often controlled where humans settled and played a pivotal role in their overall social and economic prosperity.

Water in Ancient Civilizations

Around the world, freshwater resources provided a degree of stability that influenced the growth of a number of ancient civilizations. While the presence of sufficient freshwater did not solve problems directly, it did do two things: 1) It improved the health of residents through better hygiene and hydration, and 2) it alleviated food shortages through crop irrigation practices.

Approximately 7,000 years ago, small settlements in the Middle East in a region called Mesopotamia (modern-day Iraq and Syria) began to develop the first organized agrarian communities in the rich soils of the alluvial plains within the watershed of the Tigris and Euphrates rivers.

During the Ubaid Period (5900 to 4000 B.C.E.), high water tables helped bring prosperity to these agricultural communities by enabling them to develop the earliest community irrigation systems for watering crops. By 4700 B.C.E., a number of large villages were constructed, most built with bricks made from clay. The residents designed and built underground water storage systems, engineered a number of new farming tools, refined work with the wheel, and produced some of the earliest written languages.

This considerable growth and innovation was later named a Cradle of Civilization and was repeated in several other locations around the world. Such regional communities grew and flourished mainly due to an abundance of freshwater. In fact, ample freshwater, leading to agricultural prosperity, historically has enabled many residents of a society to then focus their energies on developments in architecture, the arts, education, the natural sciences, and technology.

Lush farms and forests supported the Nile River Valley during the construction of the Egyptian pyramids between 3000 and 2150 B.C.E. Water was needed to grow crops to feed the tens of thousands of laborers who built at least 138 of these unique, large stone structures. In fact, the flooding of the Nile River during this time allowed for the transport (floated on flat barges) of much of the stone used for the pyramids.

For most ancient nations, early travel and commerce relied on a network of rivers and tributaries. The Mayan civilization occupied a major portion of what is today known as Central America, including Belize, El Salvador, Guatemala, and western Honduras. Communities in this region used long boats to travel throughout the network of rivers in the tropical lowlands and developed sophisticated irrigation systems to grow crops in previously arid regions. Between 250 and 900 B.C.E., many large temples and structures were built, incorporating elements of spirituality, such as Chac, the god of rain, whom citizens would pray to for abundant moisture for their crops.

The Age of Emperors in China was centered around a series of settlements along the Yangzte River and Yellow River basins. The Xia Dynasty (2070 to 1600 B.C.E.) was one of the first formal governments in the region; it was known to have used a number of engineering efforts, such as earthen dikes, to halt seasonal flooding along the Yellow River.

The Great Wall of China, spanning nearly 4,000 miles (6,437 kilometers) across the country, was built to protect an abundance of freshwater and its adjacent lands. Led by the Qin Dynasty beginning in 220 B.C.E., tens of thousands of workers used rock, mortar, and earth to assemble this structure to keep out invading Xiongnu nomads. The construction of the Great Wall relied on water on many levels: to grow food, to hydrate workers, and to mix mortar as cement to build the structure.

In these and other locations around the planet, early advanced settlements studied water and began to explain its scientific properties, as well as its relationship to the land and atmosphere. The Greek philosopher Thales (624–526 B.C.E.) was one of the earliest individuals to make scientific observations about water and life. Often criticized by his peers based on how locals perceived his far-ranging theories, Thales thought that the Earth floated on water and that the liquid caused numerous natural events, including earthquakes. Thales concluded that water was the "principle whence all things in the universe spring."

A follower of Thales, Anaximander (611–547 B.C.E.), described elements of what would become known as the water cycle: "From whence all things flow, and into the same are corrupted; hence it is that infinite worlds are framed, and those vanish again into that whence they have the original." Years later, the philosophers Aristotle, Socrates, and Plato all built on Thales's scientific work, concluding that all life emerged from water.

Water in Modern Times

The Industrial Revolution in Europe circa 1700 brought an unprecedented period of rapid economic growth that relied on a considerable supply of freshwater. Water was required to complete manufacturing tasks, as well as to support the day-to-day needs of a growing population.

The eighteenth century witnessed a widespread movement of people, from rural areas into cities, seeking higher paid employment. Larger cities built bigger water transport systems that brought freshwater to factories and homes. This infrastructure was replicated across African, Asian, Australian, North American, Russian, and South American settlements well into the twenty-first century.

Water plays an essential role in modern society. It is used to irrigate crops. It is processed into safe drinking water, and piping systems enable the removal of household waste streams with water. It cools the power plants that supply the world with electricity. Commerce relies on it for portions of the global economy for essential transport. It is used in almost every manufacturing process, including the assembly of hundreds of millions of sophisticated computer chips.

Freshwater Consumption

Up to 3.57 quadrillion gallons (13.5 quadrillion liters) of freshwater is consumed worldwide per year. This water use can be broken down by average percentage in three categories: agriculture (70 percent), business and industry (18 percent), and domestic use (12 percent).

During the twentieth century, freshwater consumption grew sixfold, far outpacing the tripling of the global human population. There are two vastly different water consumption worlds. The first one exists throughout the mostly rural and underdeveloped areas of Africa, Asia, and South America. Individual use may include ingestion of 0.25 gallon (1 liter) of water and use of less than 20 gallons (76 liters) per day per person.

In more developed communities in China, Europe, and North America, water consumption increases substantially. Total combined household and community use can exceed 1,560 gallons (5,905 liters) per day per person. Individuals in these countries consume up to 1 gallon (3.8 liters) and use 110 gallons (416 liters) in the household per day. Industrial and sewage facilities utilize 800 gallons (3,028 liters), and 650 gallons (2,461 liters) are distributed to irrigate farm crops, supplementing low precipitation levels. Intensive farming uses up to 75 percent of local water supplies. Approximately 305 million U.S. residents used an estimated 425 billion gallons (1,609 billion liters) of freshwater per day in 2008.

There is a great variance of water supply and usage patterns among the continents. Landmass size is one factor. For example, Asia is approximately five and a half times larger than Australia and therefore contains greater water resources. Because the northern continents contain more landmass than the southern ones, they also contain a larger supply of freshwater.

Precipitation levels also determine freshwater availability. The greatest water supply is in South America, where 8 trillion gallons (30 trillion liters) per day is available. This is due to South America hosting the largest tropical rain forests in the world, which receive upwards of 350 inches (889 centimeters) of precipitation per year. By comparison, more than half of Africa receives less than 20 inches of rain (51 centimeters) per year.

Utilization of water depends on population and the size of agriculture and industry. Out of all continental areas, Asia performs the most manufacturing, as well as irrigation, topping 1 trillion gallons (3.8 trillion liters) of water use per day. The highest freshwater use by individuals occurs in North America, where between 1,000 and 1,600 gallons (3,785 to 6,057 liters) is used per person daily (this includes the water used for growing food and processing waste).

According to the United Nations World Water Assessment Program, the minimum amount of water needed for an individual is between 5 and 10 gallons (19 and 38 liters) a day, and 1 billion people lack access to sufficient clean water worldwide. The United Nations has forecasted that the consumption of freshwater to meet social and economic demands will have grown by 24 percent by 2025, and 1.8 billion people will lack adequate freshwater.

Centralized Public Water Systems

At the turn of the twentieth century, the world contained a population of more than 1.5 billion people who consumed approximately 221 cubic miles (921 cubic kilometers) of freshwater annually. By 2009, that population had climbed to 6.7 billion people, and freshwater use had soared fourfold to 887 cubic miles (3,697 cubic kilometers) per year. This desire for more water has, in turn, led to multibillion-dollar investments to pump, treat, and distribute ample freshwater directly to faucets.

Public freshwater is typically delivered by a government entity; however, since the 1990s private suppliers have become more common. Water is transported through three methods: surface transport using natural rivers, lakes, or streams; surface canals and piping or reservoirs built by humans; and underground piping and aboveground storage (water towers). A community may rely on a combination of these methods to meet its needs.

Today's modern engineering systems have resulted in the efficient movement of water across great distances. Most of these systems are incredibly large, carrying hundreds of millions of gallons across hundreds of miles of piping to tens of millions of city residents. Approximately 84 percent of the residents of the United States rely on such public water supply systems.

Around the world, governments provide a high percentage of public water to their residents. Populations that have a particularly high dependency on public water systems include 92 percent of those living in Armenia, 91 percent of the citizens of Cuba, and 87 percent of the population of South Africa.

Many nations, however, lack a modern water distribution system that is large enough for the entire country. Those countries that lack sufficient public water systems and still depend on local wells include Romania (57 percent of the population), Zambia (55 percent), Madagascar (45 percent), Ethiopia (22

TORONTO AND LAKE ONTARIO

The modern public water system in the city of Toronto, Canada, relies on both chemistry and engineering to deliver safe water to 2.5 million residents. This community of 243 square miles (629 square kilometers) sits at the edge of Lake Ontario, the smallest of the five Great Lakes of North America, and utilizes the 7,540-square-mile (19,529-square-kilometer) lake for all its freshwater needs.

Toronto uses a complex treatment and distribution system comprised of four filtration plants, eighteen pumping stations, ten reservoirs, 316 miles (508 kilometers) of trunk pipes, and 3,116 miles (5,014 kilometers) of distribution pipes to take relatively moderate-quality lake water and filter and treat it with chlorine and other chemicals to provide high-quality, safe drinking water. This requires 1,546 full-time employees.

In 2007, this system produced up to 700 million gallons (2,650 million liters) per day. As of 2007, the cost, per family, was approximately $535.44 per year for water and sewer fees. Water use in the region grew at around 9 percent per year between 2006 and 2009.

percent), and Afghanistan (13 percent). While local wells can provide sufficient freshwater supplies in some countries for limited populations, they are not as deep as the public groundwater wells (tapping into larger water supplies) and also are not required to meet the more stringent government standards for chemical composition and pollutants.

Freshwater Pollution

Although the European industrial revolution brought great prosperity to multiple nations, many environmental and health problems arose from the intensive use and pollution of freshwater. Waste streams polluting freshwater sources included untreated human and animal sewage and industrial discharges (containing solvents such as paints, dyes, metals, and oil). Many complex chemical industrial by-products in water-based liquid solutions simply were deposited directly into the closest water bodies, such as lakes, rivers, oceans, or old wells, without consideration. This practice was called the dilution method due to the premise that larger freshwater sources made pollution less harmful.

In the nineteenth century, the quality of life for many residents in cities, such as London, Paris, Berlin, and Madrid, reached new highs. At the same time, serious environmental problems began to arise in relation to polluted freshwater systems.

When a large outbreak of cholera, a potentially fatal intestinal disease, occurred in London, England, in 1854, British physician John Snow found that it had originated in wells that had been polluted with human waste. Within a year 14,137 people had died. Snow's sampling of water supplies revealed elevated levels of bacteria that had thrived on human waste. He proved that certain bacteria-reliant diseases, such as cholera, are distributed in the water. Previously, public health officials had believed that all disease was transported through the air. Snow's contributions launched the science of epidemiology and methods for tracking pollutants in freshwater sources.

In the mid-twentieth-century United States, many Americans were enjoying great economic prosperity. It was during this period—despite all that was known about the relationship between the freshwater supply and public health—that freshwater pollution reached an apex in the United States.

On June 22, 1969, the Cuyahoga River in Cleveland, Ohio, was set ablaze by a railroad accident over the water, and a massive fire burned on the surface of the river for hours. Since 1936, this 100-mile-long (161-kilometer-long) river had experienced numerous fires from spilled petrochemical and other industrial pollution. The five-story-high flames in the 1969 fire could be seen for miles, and toxic odors drifted far upriver and downriver. This incident received national attention and revealed a major gap in regulatory oversight of freshwater pollution.

Although many states, such as New York and Illinois, had made significant investments between 1900 and 1950 to treat sewage and build major water delivery networks, many communities lagged behind. Within a year of the Cuyahoga fire, a shift in the federal government's environmental policy resulted in landmark legislation from the U.S. Congress. The Water Pollution Control Act was passed in 1972 (it was later amended to form the Clean Water Act in 1977), delivering funding for many towns and cities to build municipal wastewater treatment plants and establishing uniform standards to protect freshwater. Regulations were imposed on companies either to treat or to dispose of industrial waste with a specific permit from the government to reduce biological pollution. Within a decade, many bodies of water where swimming and fishing had been banned were cleaner, and some even reopened to the public.

Years later, in 2002, the U.S. Environmental Protection Agency (EPA), a government agency charged with setting national environmental standards and regulations, categorized the Cuyahoga a "River Area of Concern" due to its industrial-waste discharges and urban storm water runoff, even after the waterway was named an American Heritage River in 1998 in recognition of broad cleanup efforts. Ongoing remediation projects continue to tackle river pollution in this heavily industrial part of Ohio.

Freshwater use patterns in the early twenty-first century have shifted globally as manufacturing centers have moved from North America and Europe to Asia. In the late 1990s, entirely new industrial cities arose across southern China, resulting in measurable changes in water use and pollution patterns. A 2003 United Nations survey of Asian rivers found that increased industrial activity has resulted in surface waters holding twenty times more lead than in Western countries, four times as many suspended solids, and three times as much bacteria from untreated human waste.

By contrast, in the United States and central and western Europe, economic changes centered around a decline in manufacturing have led to reduced business water consumption—and therefore a reduction in the corresponding pollution levels. For example, in one location, the Republic of Moldova, industrial water use decreased by 54 percent, from 809,748 gallons (3.1 million liters) per day in 1990 to 373,730 gallons (1.4 million liters) per day in 1999.

In the United States, manufacturing employed 25 percent of the population in 1970; by 2005, that number had shrunk to less than 10 percent. This has resulted in a decline, by almost a third, in industrial freshwater use. The U.S. Environmental Protection Agency, which tracks some 650 different chemical pollutants that are released by 21,000 facilities nationwide, reported in 2009 that

In this picture from 1968, three men in a motorboat take water samples on the Cuyahoga River near Jaite, Ohio, where junk cars had been dumped into the waterway. A major fire took place in this area in June 1969 after accumulating industrial discharges were ignited by a train accident. Many credit the fire and the resulting media coverage as being motivating forces behind the passage of the federal Clean Water Act in 1972 and the creation of agencies such as the U.S. Environmental Protection Agency. *(Alfred Eisenstaedt/ Time & Life Pictures/Getty Images)*

freshwater pollution had declined for the third year in a row, and that it was down more than 12 percent since 2005.

Nevertheless, water pollution is an ongoing challenge across the globe. According to the World Water Council, an international organization based in Marseilles, France, that works to improve access to clean water, waterborne diseases are a severe problem for many less developed countries. Two in ten people do not have access to safe freshwater. As many as 41,095 children die every day from bacterial diseases obtained from unsafe water.

According to the United Nations, the number of such deaths is projected to increase as the population grows. In addition, in 2008 there were roughly 705 million people with no access to clean freshwater, spread across 350 low-income and 355 middle-income global locations. By 2050, it is estimated that up to 30 percent of the world's population will face chronic and severe water shortages.

Stresses on the Freshwater Supply

As the human population has grown steadily since the early twentieth century, so has the thirst for considerably more freshwater. Estimated worldwide total groundwater supplies declined 30 percent between 1970 and 2000, due to increased withdrawals, mostly by growing cities and expanded farms. Additionally, by 2004, up to 35 percent of worldwide available freshwater from lakes, rivers, and underground sources had been depleted by humans.

This has resulted in obvious limits on the availability of freshwater, especially in large and arid communities. In 2008, forty countries faced particularly acute water shortages, including Barbados, Cyprus, Israel, Libya, Rwanda, and Trinidad. Island nations and those surrounded by desert are more commonly impacted by periods of low rainfall and limited or salt-contaminated groundwater tables. Many houses rely on capture of rain into large containers or cisterns for future use. Other wider geographical areas such as southern Africa, northern Asia, central Australia, northern Mexico, western Pakistan, and the western United States have had to function with insufficient local freshwater supplies for generations.

If all the rain that occurs worldwide each year were spread evenly across the planet, it would create a 34-inch-deep (86-centimeter-deep) body of freshwater. Precipitation, however, does not fall this way. The irregular placement of rain and

GEOGRAPHIC REGIONS WITH FRESHWATER CHALLENGES

Region	Percent of Population with Public Water Supplies	Percent of Population with Wells or Other Water Supplies	Percent of Population with No Improved Water Supplies
Sub-Saharan Africa	16	42	42
South Asia	22	65	13
Southeast Asia	32	54	14
Eastern Asia	73	15	12
Oceania	73	21	6
Northern Africa	78	14	8
Western Asia	80	10	10
Latin America/Caribbean	80	12	8
Developed Nations	93	6	1

Source: Progress on Drinking Water and Sanitation. UNICEF and the World Health Organization, 2008.

runoff has resulted in an ongoing crisis in many communities. Approximately 16 percent of the world population does not have regular access to sufficient and reliably clean water.

In some communities with limited water, agricultural removals take up to 90 percent of the freshwater from residents. One example of large-scale agricultural water use is a 9,500-mile-long (15,286-kilometer-long) section of land from Morocco in North Africa across Egypt through the Middle East and into northern China. This region has been particularly hard-hit by droughts that, in concert with growing water use patterns, have resulted in a historic decrease in groundwater availability.

In response to reduced groundwater and surface water supplies, in 2002 the Chinese government undertook a massive engineering project to divert portions of the Yangtze River and use a series of canals to redeposit the water into the Yellow River, which periodically runs dry across northern China. China's officials have recognized the northern regions—which make up 64 percent of the nation's landmass—as experiencing a crisis of freshwater shortages. Water tables have dropped as much as 20 feet (6 meters) in a single year in northern cities. The $50-billion project, which could divert up to 1.2 trillion gallons (4.5 trillion liters) of water per year and includes the construction of the Three Gorges Dam (with a power generating capacity of 22,500 megawatts, it is the largest dam on Earth) on the Yangtze River, might take more than three decades to complete.

Another example of freshwater depletion can be found in the small nation of Nepal, located in the central Himalayas on the northern boundary of India. An estimated 1.8 million people live in the Kathmandu Valley. In this city center, population growth in 2008 was at almost 7 percent. Water demands had peaked at 30 million gallons (114 million liters) per day, although only 32 million gallons (121 million liters) are available in the wet season and 22 million gallons (83 million liters) in the dry season. Although 70 percent of the population has access to piped water, it is not necessarily potable. In addition, when too much water is removed from groundwater sources, it results in a lowering of the water table, a reduction in water quality, and changes in the natural ecosystems.

The Nepalese government has undertaken a number of efforts to address freshwater shortages, including conservation programs, repairs to leaks in the supply system, and seeking new inventories of groundwater supplies. In 2009, the government proposed a series of new reservoirs, water treatment plants, and upgraded piping networks, but these may take years to build, and the cost is projected to exceed $500 million.

Some of the more arid communities that have exceeded their capacities of freshwater sources are very wealthy. This has resulted in significant, and often very expensive, efforts to secure adequate freshwater supplies. For instance, the wealthy Middle Eastern nation of Dubai, located in the United Arab

Emirates, has used immense monetary resources to build a world-class city in the Arabian Desert at the edge of the Persian Gulf. As the population of Dubai City has grown to more than 2.2 million, so has its skyline, which is full of multi-story buildings.

This arid climate receives less than 6 inches (15 centimeters) of rain per year, and temperatures often exceed 105 degrees Fahrenheit (41 degrees Celsius).

PROFILE OF A U.S. TOWN WATER DEPARTMENT

In the U.S. state of Massachusetts, one municipal water department provides an example of an operation dedicated to providing safe freshwater to the public.

Bordered on two sides by the Atlantic Ocean and the Cape Cod Bay, the 21-square-mile (54-square-kilometer) coastal town of Orleans has roughly 6,324 year-round residents. It also has only one source of freshwater—a single underground aquifer held in place by the contours of the land and buffered by the ring of salt water surrounding Cape Cod. In this area, digging wells was the historic method for accessing freshwater; groundwater access begins at approximately 20 feet (6 meters) below the surface.

In 1962, the town of Orleans began providing residents with treated water via a public water supply system. By 2009, 99 percent of the residents relied on this water supply. The Orleans Water Department has a modern water treatment plant and seven groundwater wells located in South Orleans. The town owns 538 acres (218 hectares) of land that surround the wellheads to protect the water supply from pollution. Once water is ready for distribution, it can be temporarily stored in one of two large water tanks that hold a total of 3 million gallons (11 million liters).

The water department bills residents based on their water usage. Up to half the population uses less than 30,000 gallons (113,562 liters) per year, costing approximately $180 annually per household. The highest users, such as larger homes and businesses, which make up less than 15 percent of the properties, require more than 100,000 gallons (378,541 liters) per year; this level of usage can cost upwards of $1,298 annually.

Efforts to pump water from underground wells have lowered the water tables to the point where groundwater has been contaminated with salt. Currently, the main water supply for residents is derived from desalination plants that remove salt water from the Persian Gulf and turn it into potable freshwater. As of 2009, the government of Dubai is building three concrete underground water reservoirs in the adjacent desert to hold 850 million gallons (3,218 million liters) of freshwater.

There also is a major seasonal variance in water use: In 2008, residents of Orleans used a total of approximately 500,000 gallons (1.9 million liters) of water per day in the winter and approximately 2.2 million gallons (8.3 million liters) per day in the summer. In all, 337 million gallons (1,276 million liters) of water were consumed in 2008.

The water treatment plant was upgraded in 2005 with a $6 million, state-of-the-art membrane filtration system that captures the iron and manganese deposits that build up naturally in the aquifer. An annual report required by the federal and state governments details water quality results. Orleans sometimes shows very low amounts of substances such as chlorine, coliform bacteria, copper, nitrate, radium, sodium, sulfate, and other organic or inorganic substances, but none have exceeded government standards for health and safety since the mid-1990s.

Such freshwater public distribution systems can be complex and costly. The town of Orleans has built a respectable infrastructure, which includes more than 109 miles (175 kilometers) of water pipes. The water plant's biggest expense, after paying salaries for nine employees (totaling $420,000 in 2008), is paying for electricity to pump the water through the pipes to households and residences, a total cost of $120,000 per year.

Automated computer systems track every facet of the system, helping the town to manage costs. The town also is looking into installing a wind turbine in order to use renewable energy to offset high power costs.

These reservoirs, which are sheltered from the heat and winds, lower the massive rate of evaporation.

As technology has advanced worldwide, the amount of freshwater needed by the international manufacturing industry has grown. In just one example of industrial water consumption, the latest model of computer laptop requires 30,000 gallons (113,562 liters) of water to manufacture all of its parts.

Additionally, as the number of farms has grown rapidly to meet food demands, agriculture is performed in more and more regions that do not receive sufficient natural irrigation. The use of up to 90 percent of the public treated water puts stress on the system. A single pound of rice can require 600 gallons (2,271 liters) of water, and a pound of wheat takes 130 gallons (492 liters).

Some communities, especially those with "surplus" water supplies, have been slow to make water efficiency and conservation a priority. Up until 1986, water costs in New York City often were based on an average household usage. If one residence used 2,000 gallons (7,571 liters) per month and the other used 6,000 gallons (22,712 liters), both paid the same water rate. Only since 1987 has the city

An oversized truck dumps a load of rock across the remaining section of a diversion canal linked to China's Yangtze River in November 2002, marking another stage in the completion of the massive and yet controversial Three Gorges Dam project. The $32 billion South-North Diversion Project began in 1994, and the dam is expected to be fully operational by 2011. It is anticipated to run thirty-two hydroelectric turbines and generate up to 22,500 megawatts of power. *(Stringer/AFP/Getty Images)*

DAILY HOUSEHOLD WATER USE IN THE UNITED STATES
(Breakdown of 400 gallons used on average by a family of four)

Fixture/Appliance	By Percent	Water Used	Action
Bathroom Sink	7.7	5 to 12 gallons	Brush teeth, wash hands and face, and shave.
Kitchen Sink	8.0	10 to 30 gallons	Washing dishes from one meal by hand.
Shower	16.8	20 to 45 gallons	Range based on shower head and length and intensity of shower.
Washing Machine	21.7	20 to 40 gallons	Per load of clothes.
Toilet	26.7	1 to 6 gallons	Per flush.
Other (such as leaks and outdoor use)	19.1	30 to 55 gallons	Water system leaks, garden use, washing a car, and so on.

Source: Water Sense. U.S. Environmental Protection Agency, 2008.

water department installed wired meters to determine actual usage at individual residences and charged according to water used. Now the department is in the midst of a project to install 826,000 wireless meters by 2011 in order to improve the accuracy of property usage.

Communities dealing with water scarcity also have implemented measures to update residential fixtures such as toilets, showers, and sinks to reduce usage. The city of Fukuoka, Japan, is located in the southern portion of the island nation and counted approximately 1.4 million residents in 2006. In 1978, a major drought led the government to strictly control water use in the area. By 2005, conservation measures had been implemented in 96 percent of households, saving more than 275 gallons (1,041 liters) on average in each home or 54 million gallons (204 million liters) citywide each month. Despite a 30 percent increase in the population since 1978, total water use has dropped by 20 percent.

Climate change also is imposing considerable stress on freshwater supplies. In 2007, the Intergovernmental Panel on Climate Change, the United Nations–established body for the assessment of global climate change, estimated that worldwide average temperatures will increase between 1.8 and 5.2 degrees Fahrenheit (3.2 and 9.4 degrees Celsius) by 2100. Because climate is the main factor in the planetary hydrologic cycle, this increase potentially could upset typical weather and precipitation patterns. An increase in temperature could result in either fewer or greater storms, with less or more rain and snow.

This change in precipitation could apply new pressures to the freshwater supply, including severely depleted groundwater levels. Some areas will become much wetter than they are now, and others will become desert-like. Two early results of global warming include the shrinkage of the glaciers on top of Africa's Mount Kilimanjaro, which have lost 73 percent of their mass since the 1970s, and a five-year drought in the South American Amazon River basin, resulting in a lowering of river levels by as much as 30 feet (9 meters) in some places.

Selected Web Sites

Cuyahoga River Area of Concern, U.S. Environmental Protection Agency: http://www.epa.gov/glnpo/aoc/cuyahoga.html.

Distribution of Earth's Water, U.S. Geological Survey: http://ga.water.usgs.gov/edu/waterdistribution.html.

International Decade for Action, Water for Life (2005–2015): http://www.un.org/waterforlifedecade/.

United Nations World Water Assessment Program: http://www.unesco.org/water/wwap/.

World Water Council: http://www.worldwatercouncil.org.

Pacific Institute, The World's Water: http://www.worldwater.org.

Further Reading

Day, Trevor. *Water.* New York: DK, 2007.

Glennon, Robert. *Water Follies.* Washington, DC: Island, 2002.

Goudie, Andrew. *The Human Impact on the Natural Environment.* Malden, MA: Blackwell, 2000.

Kumagai, Michio, and Warwick F. Vincent, eds. *Freshwater Management.* New York: Springer-Verlag, 2005.

Marks, William E., ed. *Water Voices from Around the World.* Edgartown, MA: Water Voice, 2007.

United Nations. *World Water Development Report: Water for People, Water for Life.* Barcelona, Spain: Berghahn, 2003.

Ward, Andy D. *Environmental Hydrology.* Boca Raton, FL: Lewis, 2004.

GLOBAL FRESHWATER
CASE STUDIES

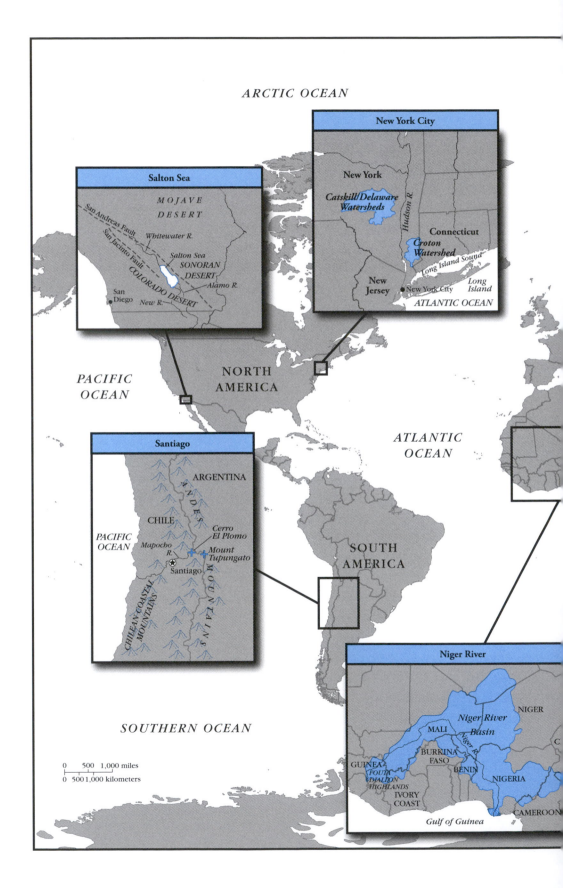

Salton Sea

MOJAVE DESERT

San Andreas Fault

Whitewater R.

San Jacinto Fault

Salton Sea

SONORAN DESERT

COLORADO DESERT

Alamo R.

San Diego

New R.

New York City

New York

Catskill/Delaware Watersheds

Hudson R.

Connecticut

Croton Watershed

Long Island Sound

New Jersey

New York City

Long Island

ATLANTIC OCEAN

Santiago

ARGENTINA

A N D E S

CHILE

Cerro El Plomo

Mapocho R.

Mount Tupungato

PACIFIC OCEAN

Santiago

CHILEAN COASTAL MOUNTAINS

M O U N T A I N S

Niger River

NIGER

Niger River Basin

MALI

Niger R.

BURKINA FASO

BENIN

NIGERIA

GUINEA

FOUTA DJALLON HIGHLANDS

IVORY COAST

CAMEROON

Gulf of Guinea

ARCTIC OCEAN

NORTH AMERICA

PACIFIC OCEAN

ATLANTIC OCEAN

SOUTH AMERICA

SOUTHERN OCEAN

0 500 1,000 miles

0 500 1,000 kilometers

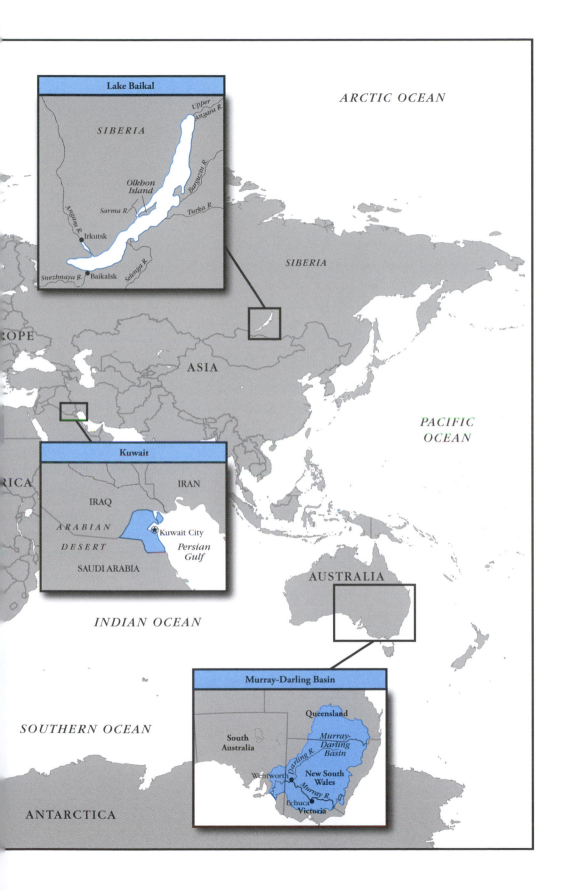

Lake Baikal

SIBERIA

Upper
Angara R.

Olkhon
Island

Barguzin R.

Sarma R.

Turka R.

Angara R.

Irkutsk

Snezhnaya R.   Baikalsk

Selenga R.

SIBERIA

ARCTIC OCEAN

ASIA

PACIFIC
OCEAN

Kuwait

IRAN

IRAQ

ARABIAN

DESERT   Kuwait City

Persian
Gulf

SAUDI ARABIA

AUSTRALIA

ROPE

RICA

INDIAN OCEAN

SOUTHERN OCEAN

ANTARCTICA

Murray-Darling Basin

Queensland

South
Australia

Murray-
Darling
Basin

Darling R.

Wentworth

New South
Wales

Murray R.

Echuca

Victoria

3 Salton Sea California

Nestled in a valley surrounded by the Mojave Desert to the north, the Sonoran Desert to the east and south, and the Colorado Desert to the west is a distinctive body of water called the Salton Sea. Located 80 miles (129 kilometers) east of San Diego, California, this body of water sits 220 feet (67 meters) below sea level in an ancient lake bed.

The Salton Sea is 35 miles (56 kilometers) long north to south by 15 miles (24 kilometers) wide west to east, and it is the largest lake in California. It averages 29 feet (8.8 meters) deep with a maximum depth of 51 feet (16 meters); however, this lake has a long history of fluctuating water levels. It most recently filled in 1905 when a flood broke through a levee transporting water from the Colorado River. Rushing northward, freshwater poured into the lake until 1907, increasing its size to more than 500 square miles (1,295 square kilometers).

Although the Salton Sea provides a welcome haven for birds and other wildlife living along the Pacific flyways, the lack of a water outlet, less than 4 inches (10 centimeters) of annual rainfall, year-round strong desert winds, and summer air temperatures that often exceed 120 degrees Fahrenheit (49 degrees Celsius) make living conditions in the area difficult for wildlife and humans alike.

This low-lying area also is tucked between the San Andreas Fault to the east and the San Jacinto Fault to the west, making the Salton Sea and its surrounding region a potentially active seismic location. Geologists have predicted that a very large earthquake will originate on the eastern edge of this large water body within the next few hundred years.

History and Ecology

The Salton Sea has a unique hydrology and geologic history. Up to a million years ago, the Colorado River emptied into the Gulf of California where Yuma, Arizona, is today. Years upon years of silt deposition from the Colorado River built a westward-moving delta of deposition. Eventually, the new land stretched 70 miles (113 kilometers) in length and closed off the northern end of the Gulf of California.

Part of this new landmass contained a large depression called the Salton Sink. It became flooded with freshwater but, with no permanent inlet or outlet, eventually dried up. For centuries, it sat dry, framed by the Chocolate Mountains to the southeast and the Little San Bernardino Mountains to the north. Then, sometime in the eighth century, the Colorado River changed its track again and began flowing into the Salton Sink once more. The new body of water, called Lake Cahuilla, grew so large that it rose above its own banks and eventually flowed to the Gulf of California.

Archeologists have uncovered evidence of Native American fishing settlements along the lake's shores that date back to between 1000 and 1400 C.E. How-

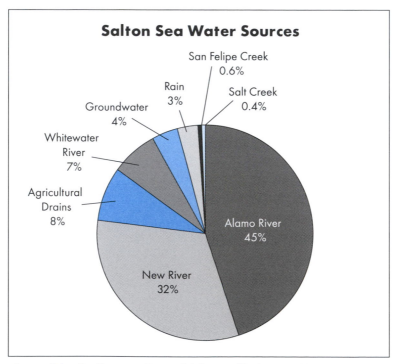

Source: Salton Sea Restoration Project, U.S. Bureau of Reclamation, 2007.

BIRDS OF THE SALTON SEA

Common Name	Scientific Name	Characteristics
American White Pelican	*Pelecanus erythrorhynchos*	Up to 80 percent of this species resides in the Salton Basin. Adults can consume up to 4 pounds of fish per day.
California Brown Pelican	*Pelecanus occidentalis californicus*	Lives mainly in open waters. This marine species has a 1-foot-long (0.3-meter-long) bill and has been endangered since 1970.
California Least Tern	*Sterna antillarum browni*	Occupying the shorelines of the Salton Sea, this endangered species feeds in shallow waters, generally staying away from humans.
Double-crested Cormorant	*Phalacrocorax auritus*	A diving species, known for an oddly bent neck and a habit of drying its wings before flying.
Osprey	*Pandion haliaetus*	Known as a fish hawk, this bird dives from the air to scoop fish from the surface with its sharp talons.
Western Snowy Plover	*Charadrius alexandrinus nivosus*	This threatened species lives in solitary sections of Salton Sea mudflats.

Source: Final Environmental Impact Report. Salton Sea Authority, 2000.

ever, once again, the Colorado changed course around the middle of the eighth century and abandoned the Salton Sink, eventually leaving the lake bed dry, until 1905 when the flood refilled it.

At the turn of the twentieth century, the most recent formation of this freshwater body resulted in beneficial environmental circumstances. Within months of its creation, the Salton Sea was a magnet for a wide range of animals, especially traveling bird species cruising across adjacent desert terrain. As many as 400 species of birds visit the lake today, and two-thirds of the birds that migrate along the Pacific Flyway stop there along their travels.

Animals that live in the Salton basin include twenty-four species of reptiles, including the gopher snake (*Pituophis catenifer*); twenty species of mammals, such as the Merriam's Kangaroo Rat (*Dipodomys merriami*); and a variety of fish species. Fish species include the sargo (*Anisotremus davidsonii*) and orangemouth corvine (*Cynoscion xanthulus*); the most common fish in these waters is the tilapia (*Oreochromis sp.*), which has a population of almost 90 million.

Human Uses

When gold seekers arrived in southern California in the 1840s, they began to scour the landscape for precious metals and mineral deposits. Arriving in the Salton Sink, they found a massive dried lake bed—potentially an ideal place for locating precious metals. However, the conditions were less than favorable. Little to no water was available in the area, and the several-day journey in and out of the valley taxed their water supply, animals, and cut into any profits. After a few years of searching, the miners had found little gold in the area. The Mexicans living at the southern half of the sink called the region "The Valley of the Dead."

At the turn of the twentieth century, another band of enterprising businessmen arrived. Farm developers sought to take advantage of the good weather and nutrient-rich soil, and they began irrigating the Imperial Valley, an area southeast of the dry Salton Sink. In this desert environment, the developers formed the Imperial Irrigation District and constructed a complex network of 1,400 miles (2,253 kilometers) of freshwater distribution pipes and trenches, which was completed in 1901. The project was an immediate success, resulting in a bounty of fruits and vegetables.

But four years later, excessive silt buildup and flooding resulted in a breach of several levees. The Colorado River flowed into the Salton Sink for the first time in hundreds of years, with the inflow from this river finally halting in 1907. Believing the Salton Sea would evaporate, the U.S. government allotted a section of the lake's underwater land to the Torres Martinez Desert Cahuilla Indians, who planned to settle the area once the waters receded.

The flooding of the Salton Sea was a habitat-altering event. It provided an ample source of freshwater for public consumption, as well as a welcome source for irrigating nearby farms. Within a few years, residents came to live near this newly formed oasis.

Towns called Bombay Beach, North Shore, and Salton City sprung up. Hundreds of homes were built, and lots for thousands more were sold. The community was advertised as an affordable and accessible option for vacationing California city dwellers. Sports such as fishing, water skiing, and sailing were a welcome respite from the intense desert heat.

Pollution and Damage

After its most recent formation, the Salton Sea faced a major hydrologic problem: It no longer had suitable freshwater inflow or outflow. After levee repairs in 1907, the Colorado River inflow had been cut off. The only surface inflow was from

As the Salton Sea water level drops, the exposed lake bed quickly dries in the arid climate. Fine dust—laden with algae, minerals, and pesticides—often is carried for miles by strong windstorms, causing widespread air pollution. *(© Paper Girl/Fotolia)*

two small rivers, the New River and the Alamo River, and rainwater and surface water runoff from adjacent fields. There also was no natural outflow; the only way that water was removed was by absorption in surrounding soils, evaporation, or human usage.

By 1980, the Salton Sea began to demonstrate multiple environmental problems. Although Imperial Valley had developed into a billion-dollar-per-year agricultural powerhouse able to grow produce in all seasons by diverting Colorado River water, the groundwater and surface water runoff from farms included excessive nutrients, pesticides, and other chemicals. Additionally, the New River and Alamo River, flowing north across the U.S.-Mexican border into the southern end of the Salton Sea, were laden with untreated industrial and human waste.

Even with the inflow from the two rivers, there was little circulation or dilution of the water in the Salton Sea, and with temperatures regularly exceeding 90 degrees Fahrenheit (32 degrees Celsius), the water started to develop a toxic chemistry. As a result, living organisms began to die off. Algae blooms consumed the available oxygen, resulting in widespread fish deaths. Diseases such as botulism killed thousands of birds.

The water chemistry of the Salton also grew worse due to the natural impact of pooled water. These conditions, which occurred since the sea was formed in 1905, included high levels of dissolved minerals in the freshwater. Once the sea had formed, the presence of water and its movement had slowly dissolved previously dried basin sediments. Two minerals in particular—salts and selenium—posed serious problems. The salts, in particular, turned the freshwater into a saline brew that exceeded 46 parts per thousand (a concentration roughly 25 percent saltier than the nearby Gulf of California at 34 parts per thousand). The source of the salts, alkaline soils, had leached salts at a rate of up to 4 million tons per year.

Local residents were no longer able to ingest the water without significant and expensive desalination treatments. Increased salinity also limited the number of plant and animal species able to survive under such conditions. The widespread deaths of tens of thousands of birds and millions of fish became a regular event, leaving the entire region smelling of rot and decay. The federal government built an incinerator, often running it twenty-four hours per day, to destroy all the washed-up animal carcasses. To this day, the salinity continues to climb, and plant and animal die-offs are common.

The excess selenium also has posed problems for animal and human health. This element, which occurs in multiple forms, has a natural low level of radioactivity. When water saturated the old lake bed, selenium emerged from the soils. At first, the selenium posed no health risks. In fact, in low doses, it is beneficial for biological health. However, when the concentration exceeded 10 parts per billion, state health officials limited human ingestion of fish from

A regional stopover for migratory birds, the Salton Sea is a part-time residence for many species, including the American White Pelican (*Pelecanus erythrorhynchos*). Unfortunately, this waterway has become heavily polluted with excessive nutrients, salts, and other chemicals and is a breeding ground for a host of fish diseases, which, in turn, cause numerous birds to become ill and die each year. *(Richard Reid/National Geographic/ Getty Images)*

these waters to 8 ounces (227 grams) over a two-week period. Overexposure can result in selenosis, a disease marked by such symptoms as respiratory problems, neurological damage, numbness, and deformed hair, teeth, and bones.

By 2008, the Salton Sea had shrunk by 25 percent to 365 square miles (945 square kilometers). As the water has receded, excessive pollution has settled on the newly exposed land and the surrounding areas.

The dried earth that formerly was underwater became layered in a fine dust. This region experiences powerful desert windstorms, and when such storms blow across these areas, material is lifted thousands of feet into the sky. Tons of toxic debris, containing particles of dried algae, salts, selenium, and residual pesticides, are carried for miles in every direction, landing in nearby communities such as Palm Springs and as far away as San Diego. If water levels continue to decline, both government officials and conservationists project that this problem will grow worse.

Many Salton Sea residents have abandoned the region. The 2000 census listed a regional population of 978 (compared to six times that number in 1970). The largest town, Bombay Beach, had fewer than 312 residents in 2008. Most of the planned subdivisions are empty lots filled with overgrown desert shrubs, and many local businesses are shuttered. Dozens of waterfront structures such as hotels, yacht clubs, piers, jetties, and docks are stranded inland as water levels continue to descend. Even the grass on the once-popular golf course is long gone, replaced with acres of sandy terrain.

The management of Salton Sea has become one of the most intensely debated issues for a freshwater location in the western United States. More than once, government bureaucrats have tried to address the issues of the reduced water quality resulting in large bird and fish kills and other damage to the eco-system. Many restoration ideas have been discussed, but due to disagreements, considerable mitigation costs, and political infighting, no comprehensive plan has been implemented.

Mitigation and Management

In 1930, the U.S. government created the 38,000-acre (15,378-hectare) Salton Sea National Wildlife Refuge (now called the Sonny Bono Salton Sea National Wildlife Refuge) in the southern portion of the area, 40 miles (64 kilometers) from the Mexican border. More than 95 percent of the refuge consists of open water, which is fed mostly by agricultural runoff from the Imperial Valley. In the 1950s, a plan was discussed to import lower salinity seawater from the Gulf of California to improve the sea's water quality and export low-quality Salton Sea water, but the plan was rejected as being too costly.

In 1993, the Salton Sea Authority, a governmental organization consisting of Native American, water district, and county representatives, was created to revitalize the region. In 1998, the U.S. Congress passed the Salton Sea Reclamation Act to study options for managing the salinity and elevation of the sea to improve fish and wildlife health.

In 2000, the Salton Sea Authority developed an Environmental Impact Report, presenting several options for restoration. The preferred recommendation was to build a $750 million dam to split the Salton Sea in two. According to this proposal, one half would remain open water; the other half would become dried lake bed and isolated wetlands. This would allow the sea to improve in water quality over time, while accepting the fact that the eventual fate of a portion of the basin was to become dried lake bed. Ten years later, this plan still was being debated by multiple stakeholders, and no action had been taken.

The debate over what to do with the Salton is emblematic of the intense thirst for freshwater in this western region that has been raging for more than a century. California recently has admitted to using more than its allotted share of the Colorado River; in 2002, the state was forced to reduce water withdrawals from 5.2 million acre feet (6.4 billion cubic meters) per year to 4.4 million (0.5 million). In 2005, the Imperial Water District reached a fifteen-year agreement with the city of San Diego to sell the district water shares from the Colorado River, resulting in up to 20 percent less water flowing from the New River and the Alamo River to the Salton Sea. This does not bode well for the lake's future.

In 2008, the California Legislative Analyst's Office produced the report *Restoring the Salton Sea,* which recommended spending approximately $9 billion on a spectrum of preservation efforts over a twenty-five-year period. According to the proposal, which is somewhat similar to the recommendations made in 2000, the sea would be reduced to a footprint of 147 square miles (381 square kilometers), little more than half of its current size. Stone and earthen berms would form a horseshoe-shaped northern section of open water, while the southern portion would be allowed to evaporate into a cluster of smaller salty wetland communities and eventually dry lake bed. As of early 2010, the proposal had yet to be acted on by the legislature.

During its century of existence, the Salton Sea has defied predictions. Water quality has steadily declined, although some bird and fish species have continued to thrive under the nutrient-rich conditions. This cycle of ecological extremes has resulted in little long-term stability. Researchers predict that environmental conditions will become worse with less water input. The lake's surface area has declined by 8 percent since 2006, and its waters have grown 9 percent saltier. Unless considerable changes are made, this location likely will again face the fate that has been repeated at least twice in history: It will become a dried-up and dormant ancient lake bed.

Selected Web Sites

Restoring the Salton Sea Report: www.saltonsea.water.ca.gov/docs/Restoring_SS.pdf.
Salton Sea Authority: http://www.saltonsea.ca.gov.
Sonny Bono Salton Sea National Wildlife Refuge: http://www.fws.gov/saltonsea/.
U.S. Bureau of Reclamation Salton Sea: www.usbr.gov/lc/region/programs/saltonsea.html.

Further Reading

Cohen, Michael. "The Past and Future of the Salton Sea." In *The World's Water 2008–2009: The Biennial Report on Freshwater Resources,* ed. Peter H. Gleick. Washington, DC: Island, 2009.

Hurlbert, Stuart, ed. *The Salton Sea Centennial Symposium.* Dordrecht, The Netherlands: Springer, 2008.

Kennan, George. *The Salton Sea: An Account of Harriman's Fight with the Colorado River (1917).* Whitefish, MT: Kessinger, 2008.

McCarthy, Brendan. *Restoring the Salton Sea.* Sacramento: California Legislative Analyst's Office, 2008.

Patten, Michael A., Guy McCaskie, and Philip Unitt. *Birds of the Salton Sea.* Berkeley: University of California Press, 2003.

The Redlands Institute. *The Salton Sea Atlas.* Redlands, CA: University of Redlands/ ESRI Press, 2002.

4   Niger River West Africa

The Niger River is western Africa's largest freshwater body. Traveling in a backward C shape, the Niger follows a distinct path that flows first away from and then back to the Atlantic Ocean. The Niger River basin spans nine nations: Benin, Burkina Faso, Cameroon, Chad, Guinea, the Ivory Coast, Mali, Niger, and Nigeria.

Africa's third-longest river, the Niger is 2,610 miles (4,200 kilometers) long and contains a watershed spanning 817,600 square miles (2.1 million square kilometers), or 7.5 percent of the African continent. It originates at 3,000 feet (914 meters) in the Fouta Djallon Highlands in central Guinea, 140 miles (225 kilometers) east of the Atlantic Ocean.

Where it terminates, mixing with salt water in the Gulf of Guinea, the river occupies an expansive delta that spans 24,000 square miles (62,160 square kilometers) of wetlands and open water. The Niger River is the main source of freshwater for a population of approximately 130 million West Africans.

The Niger flows through several geographical areas from mountain uplands to floodplain lowlands. From the river's headwaters to where it empties into the ocean, the weather is tropical, with average daily temperatures in the upper 80s Fahrenheit (29 to 32 degrees Celsius) in the highlands and upper 60s Fahrenheit (18 to 21 degrees Celsius) in the lowlands. Precipitation varies substantially. In the northern highlands, only 14 inches (36 centimeters) of rain falls per year on average. Savanna grasslands to the east are the most common of the drier terrain. In the lower delta, up to 160 inches (406 centimeters) of rain falls annually. This region contains rain forest communities with nearly impassable tropical vegetation.

The Niger River's flow is increased by the merging of several rivers along the way, including the Bani, Benue, and Kaduna. In addition, the Niger experiences flooding in different areas during various times of the year.

June rains bring floods first to the higher elevation reaches. Between July and October, the middle sections of the river experience "white floods," called such because of lighter sediments suspended in the water. Then, in December, heavy rains result in "black floods," full of thick river bottom sediment, along the middle and lowest portions of the river. Along some parts of the river, water elevations can vary by as much as 30 feet (9 meters) between the top flood level and the dry season low-water mark.

The freshwater habitat created by the Niger supports an estimated 243 species of fish. There are twenty species that are endemic and found nowhere else on Earth. One such species is the hingemouth fish (*Phractolaemus ansorgii*), which can survive in waters with little oxygen by inflating a swim bladder and using it as a lung for several minutes at a time.

FEATURES OF THE NIGER RIVER

- With a rainy season that lasts from March through October, the Niger Basin receives up to 157 inches (399 centimeters) of rain per year.

- Total coverage of the Niger River watershed is one-third of West Africa (817,600 square miles, or 2.1 million square kilometers).

- Three major dredging efforts were performed in different locations on the lower half of the river in 1958, 1978, and 2001.

- Commercial boats can access more than 75 percent of the river to transport and market goods.

- Palm oil (produced from the fruit of palm plants grown in Niger River floodplains) was the most common export crop, until oil was discovered in the Niger River Delta in 1956.

NIGER RIVER SPECIES

Common Name	Scientific Name	Characteristics
African Spoonbill	*Platalea alba*	With a wide, spatula-like bill, this wetland bird is commonly seen across the Niger Basin feeding on fish and amphibians.
Black-crowned Crane	*Balearica pavonina*	Preferring freshwater marshes, these year-round residents rely on a diet that includes seeds, insects, and small vertebrates, such as frogs.
Roan Antelope	*Hippotragus equinus*	Displaying a notable mane down their backs, these antelope roam in medium-density woodlands, feeding on grasses and low plants.
Serval	*Felis serval*	This medium-sized wild cat weighs up to 45 pounds (20.4 kilograms) and lives in the drier savanna and low-elevation mountains.
Warthog	*Phacochoerus africanus*	Thriving in dense vegetation, these wild pigs dig roots, forage on berries, and eat tree bark.
White-winged Tern	*Chlidonias leucopterus*	This wetland bird resides in freshwater marshes in the Niger Basin during the winter months, nesting on floating debris; it migrates back to Europe or Asia for the rest of the year.

Sources: Jean Claude Olivry. *Niger River Basin.* Washington, DC: The World Bank, 2005, and *The Niger River: River of Rivers.* World Wildlife Fund, 2001.

The Niger stingray (*Dasyatis garouaensis*) is an uncommon freshwater species that has been found in the delta and the lower river. Threatened by water pollution and overfishing, this elusive species is smaller than its ocean counterparts, growing to only 15 inches (38 centimeters) wide and a few inches thick. This small size allows the stingray to successfully navigate the river topography, including variable terrain along river bottoms and submerged tree trunks and roots.

The delta, where the river meets the Atlantic Ocean, supports a rich habitat where freshwater and salt water merge. The spotted-necked otter (*Lutra maculicollis*) is a common resident, eating a diet rich in fish and crustaceans. These otters live in family groups made up of ten or more members.

The pygmy hippopotamus (*Choeropsis liberiensis*) forages only at night, leading a mostly solitary existence except to rear its young. The hippopotamus's diet features aquatic vegetation, including many grasses and leafy plants. Due to both residential and industrial development along the lower river, poaching, and pollution, fewer than 3,000 of these hippos remain in the region.

Another resident of the delta is the African manatee (*Trichechus senegalensis*). These large aquatic mammals, sometimes called sea cows due to their rounded shape and docile nature, venture dozens of miles upriver in search of vegetation that overhangs the water at the river's edge. Manatees often forage in hidden areas, such as at the bottom of channels or in the roots of a dense mangrove swamp. Adult manatees weigh over 1,000 pounds (454 kilograms) and can grow to as long as 14 feet (4 meters). Despite being protected by law because of their low population, these shy mammals still are hunted for their meat and fat due to poor enforcement practices.

Human Uses

Given the multiple ethnic communities living along its course, the river has been given multiple names in different languages. Several hundred years ago, the Tuareg, the regional nomadic people, named this river *gher n gheren* meaning "river of rivers." The name was altered over the years and shortened to *ngher*; in the 1620s, it was identified as the Niger by Portuguese mapmakers. The Nigerian people often call the river *Joliba,* meaning "great river."

The countries that the Niger River transects rely heavily on its freshwater resources. Many communities are situated adjacent to the riverbanks. A common method of local transportation in the region is by boat. Dirt roads also follow the waterway.

Moving away from the Niger River, the terrain is drier with less vegetation. Up to 63 percent of river basin residents work small farms that provide food such as fruits, beans, millet, rice, and sorghum. Low levels of rain since the 1990s have led to higher levels of abandoned farmland and elevated food insecurity. Regionally, some 3.3 million people have faced chronic food shortages.

The Nigerian economy has grown exponentially since oil was first discovered in the Niger River Delta region in 1956. Oil proceeds turned an undeveloped country with little national wealth into the world's sixth-largest oil exporter in 2007, with $55 billion of annual profit and 1,100 active wells. Five oil companies—Exxon Mobil, Chevron, Royal Dutch, Total, and Agip—have built 4,500 miles (7,241 kilometers) of pipelines and 159 oil fields, employing several thousand West Africans. Peak oil removals reached 2.5 million barrels per day in 2007.

Many of the people who live along and on the Niger River depend on it for more than just freshwater. The boats in this picture commonly serve as homes, as well as a means of transporting and storing locally made goods and produce. Unfortunately, the changing global climate and overuse of freshwater are threatening this traditional way of life by lowering water levels and reducing available freshwater for irrigating crops. *(© Jan Reinke/Fotolia)*

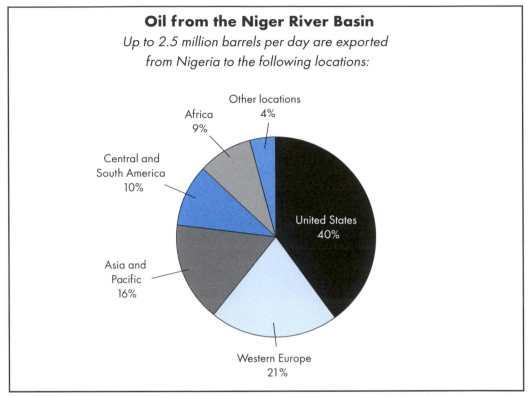

Oil from the Niger River Basin

Up to 2.5 million barrels per day are exported from Nigeria to the following locations:

- Other locations 4%
- Africa 9%
- Central and South America 10%
- Asia and Pacific 16%
- United States 40%
- Western Europe 21%

Source: Tom O'Neill "Curse of the Black Gold." *National Geographic Magazine*, February 2007.

The governments in the Niger watershed often are criticized as being corrupt. For instance, some nations, such as Nigeria, now earn up to 45 percent of their total national revenues from oil sales, but may use 30 percent or less of oil revenues to benefit the people. Instead, these nations often pour money into pet projects overseen by multiple layers of government bureaucrats. The World Bank found that in 2008, 66 percent of the population in the region suffered from poverty. The average per capita income is approximately $1,400 per year, or $1 per person per day.

The Niger Basin's steady economic growth since the late twentieth century has meant that more freshwater has been needed to generate electricity from hydro-electric dams, for irrigation systems for arid fields, and for industry to produce goods. At the same time, the region's population has increased by 3 percent per year.

Today, 80 million people depend on the Niger's freshwater for day-to-day living. Due to the surge in population, the watershed's demographics are dominated by its youth. Half of this population is made up of women and children under the age of fifteen, a fragile segment that requires considerable social service support and resources such as schools and health care facilities.

Pollution and Damage

According to the Union for African Population Studies, a nonprofit founded by the United Nations to promote scientific study of African population dynamics, since the turn of the twentieth century, West Africa has grown substantially from a population of approximately 14 million in 1900 to an estimated 130 million in 2008. The Niger River has borne the brunt of the land and water use changes, resulting in a general degradation of water quality and quantity.

The most noteworthy impact has been reduced surface flow and water availability. The Niger River's flow has declined by 55 percent since the late 1990s primarily due to reduced rainfall from weather system changes and increased withdrawals for farm irrigation.

MALARIA RESULTS IN HEAVY TOLL ACROSS THE REGION

Many West Africans living along the Niger are very poor and susceptible to a range of diseases. One of the biggest killers is malaria, which is carried in the saliva of female mosquitoes. Once a human is bitten, these miniscule parasites—100,000 of them fit on a head of a pin—swim into the bloodstream and travel to the liver where they burrow, causing a range of symptoms, including nausea, fatigue, and muscle pain, which can lead to delirium and convulsions. Up to 1 million Africans die from this disease annually.

The spread of malaria throughout West Africa has been enhanced by two variables: slum-like living conditions and the lack of adequate shelter with fine mesh screens or nets to protect people from invading bugs. The most effective method for reducing malaria has been relatively low-tech: implementing mosquito control programs. Insect breeding occurs in stagnant, freshwater pools. Improvements in ditches and waterways to increase water flow or periodic treatment with chemicals at the water's surface can lower the population of malaria-bearing mosquitoes by up to 70 percent.

Navigation by boat also has been impaired by excessive disturbances from developments such as dam building and accumulation of sediment. Many river channels that previously were known as deep-river fish habitat have become much shallower, and the change in water levels has reduced fish and plant populations.

The region's network of oil wells and interconnected pipelines encroach upon wetlands habitat along the river basin. Multiple oil spills, especially throughout the delta, have eliminated fishing grounds and destroyed hundreds of square miles of marshes and mangrove forests. Government officials have catalogued 6,817 separate spills since the late 1990s, but researchers estimate that this number may be only 20 percent of the actual total.

The expansion of petroleum facilities also has displaced entire neighborhoods in Nigeria. Violence has surged from poverty, social discontent, and ethnic conflict, and youth gangs have resorted to insurgent actions, such as kidnapping international professionals and bombing oil facilities. Between 2000 and 2006, at least seventy-five violent attacks occurred, many resulting in additional oil spills, large fires, and dozens of human fatalities.

Mitigation and Management

The Niger River is considered the "spinal column for the economy of West Africa," supporting the broad majority of resident, industry, and farming needs. In 1964, the Nigerian government formed the River Niger Commission to advance economic development goals. Sixteen years later, the river had declined greatly in quality and quantity.

In 1980, the group's name was changed to the Niger Basin Authority, in part to address the river's changing ecosystem. As of early 2010, it has nine member nations from across the basin, including Benin, Burkina Faso, Cameroon, Chad, Côte d'Ivoire, Guinea, Mali, Niger, and Nigeria. These nations work together to balance business interests and environmental efforts, including hydrologic studies, projects to reduce sedimentation, and coordinated water management programs that deal with irrigation, hydroelectric projects, and the supply of public drinking water.

To address freshwater problems using a private–public collaborative, a number of government and conservation organizations formed the Niger Basin Initiative in 2006. Consisting of groups such as the World Wildlife Fund, the Nigerian Conservation Foundation, and the Niger Basin Authority, the initiative works to maintain a healthy river system that supports plants, animals, and human needs. In order to meet this goal, the initiative created a sustainable development action plan outlining several freshwater quality improvement projects. The group plans to become involved with future business endeavors affecting the watershed to ensure that projects are ecologically sustainable and socially equitable.

In 2007, The World Bank, the largest international lender to developing countries, announced a project to address the land and water degradation trends that have occurred in the region since the late twentieth century. The Niger Basin Water Resources Development and Sustainable Ecosystem Management Program will oversee $500 million in financing to complete a number of infrastructure improvements, including improved institutional coordination of government agencies, the repair of two existing dams, better management of irrigation systems, and implementation of a watershed management plan to improve drinking water quality and availability. The governments of France and Canada, the European Commission, the African Development Bank, and The World Bank are funding the project.

Awareness of freshwater supply problems has resulted in a range of cooperative efforts. Nevertheless, the Niger River Basin, especially in the Nigerian Delta, has become a hot spot for civil unrest as residents react to the presence of international oil companies in their communities. An estimated $380 billion in oil payments to the government were stolen or wasted between 1960 and 1999. Armed rebel gangs unleashed a string of attacks on oil processing facilities and kidnapped 150 oil employees in 2007. Employers regularly travel by helicopter or armored convoy for safety. One militant group, the Movement for the Emancipation of the Niger Delta (MEND), has claimed responsibility for several attacks, threatening more aggressive tactics if oil money is not spent in a more accountable manner. A 2008 estimate of losses in oil revenues from violence over six years, from 2000 to 2006, was $750 million.

Although the conflict over oil issues continues, some freshwater enhancement projects have shown measurable progress. In 2008, the Niger Basin Authority announced an $8 billion, twenty-year plan to improve water quality and elevate flow levels of the Niger River. A portion of this money will be paid for with oil revenues.

Selected Web Sites

Niger Delta from Space: http://www.esa.int/esaEO/SEM0X632VBF_index_0.html.

Niger River After the Rainy Season: http://eosweb.larc.nasa.gov/HPDOCS/misr/misr_html/niger_river.html.

United Nations Report on the Niger River Basin: http://www.fao.org/docrep/w4347e/w4347e0i.htm.

The World Bank, Nigeria Projects: http://go.worldbank.org/4ANKR2VKI0.

World Wildlife Fund, Niger River: http://panda.org/about_our_earth/about_ freshwater/rivers/niger/.

Further Reading

Falola, Toyin, and Matthew Heaton. *A History of Nigeria.* Cambridge, UK: Cambridge University Press, 2008.

Golitzen, Katherin George, ed. *The Niger River Basin: A Vision for Sustainable Management.* Washington, DC: The World Bank, 2005.

Jenkins, Mark. *To Timbuktu: A Journey Down the Niger.* New York: Modern Times, 2008.

Watts, Michael. *Curse of the Black Gold: 50 Years of Oil in the Niger Delta.* New York: Powerhouse, 2008.

5 Lake Baikal Russia

The deepest and largest freshwater lake on the planet sits in southeastern Russia. Lake Baikal hosts depths of 5,315 feet (1,620 meters) and has a volume of 5,500 cubic miles (22,925 cubic kilometers). Forming a crescent half-moon shape, the lake is 395 miles (636 kilometers) long north to south by 30 miles (48 kilometers) wide east to west.

Baikal is surrounded by mountains, the highest being the 9,316-foot (2,840-meter) Ulan-Burgasy Range. Known as *Ozero Baykal* in Russian, this lake spans 12,200 square miles (31,598 square kilometers) of surface area with a watershed of 220,464 square miles (571,002 square kilometers), about the size of the state of Texas. It holds up to 20 percent of the total freshwater on Earth and is so deep that all five of the Great Lakes in North America could be emptied into it with room left over.

Baikal's volume of freshwater plays an influential role in local weather conditions. This region is defined by its very cold and dry winters and cool summers. It has a subarctic climate; however, such a large amount of water in one location can moderate weather systems. During the middle of winter, the lake and a 10-mile (16-kilometer) radius surrounding it may experience warmer temperatures than the surrounding area.

Despite this influence, Lake Baikal also has a very dangerous oceanic presence, in that strong weather patterns can cause significant water movement and wave action. Rapidly formed storms can intensify over open water, resulting in waves reaching 20 feet (6 meters) in height. Cold winter stretches can result in a blanket of ice that is 4 feet (1.2 meters) thick in places. Annual precipitation at

Omul (*Coregonus migratorius*), a whitefish salmon species native to Lake Baikal, is the primary catch of one of the lake's largest commercial fisheries and one of the main food resources for the people of the region. In fact, omul account for about two-thirds of all fish caught in the lake. (© Yul/Fotolia)

the north portion of the lake is approximately 14 inches (36 centimeters), while the southern section gets considerably more, roughly 36 inches (91 centimeters) per year.

Lake Baikal is much older than most lakes. Its geologic history began 80 million years ago, in the Mesozoic Era, when the region contained a subtropical valley of marshes and smaller bodies of open water that formed the habitat of dinosaurs and prehistoric plants. During that time, the collision of three tectonic plates resulted in a huge uplift that formed the Baikal, Khamar-Daban, and Primorskiy mountain ranges and a massive rift eventually formed Lake Baikal. By 30 million years ago, the lake had filled from surface water and groundwater flows to its present size.

The region is geologically active. In 1861, an earthquake killed 1,300 people and created a new 70-square-mile (181-square-kilometer) bay. Evidence of the movement of tectonic plates at the bottom of the lake also include multiple large cracks that have been found to be venting heat from the molten rock below. Annually, the lake is widening by up to 0.7 inch (2 centimeters). Geologists have theorized that the lake could be the point of origin for what will one day become a sea dividing Russia from the rest of Asia.

Both the geographical isolation and the age of Lake Baikal have allowed its animal and plant inhabitants to evolve over time as if on an island. Up to 1,700 species thrive in and around these very cold waters, including fifty species of fish, thirty-nine species of mammals, 320 species of birds, and more than 800 species of vascular plants.

Near the water's edge, evergreen trees such as the Siberian pine (*Pinus sibirica*) and Siberian larch (*Larix sibirica*) grow in shallow, low-nutrient soils. Almond willow (*Salix triandra*) and alder (*Alnus glutinosa*) emerge adjacent to wetlands in soils that are often underwater for part of the year.

Aquatic mammals include the nerpa, or Baikal seal (*Phoca sibirica*), the only freshwater seal species. With a population that may exceed 50,000, this small, steel-gray mammal consumes a diet rich in *Golomyanka,* or Baikal oilfish (*Comephorus baicalensis*).

Another lake resident, which makes up 96 percent of the zooplankton, is the tiny crustacean *Epischura baicalensis.* These shrimp-like copepods travel through

LAKE BAIKAL WATER FACTS

- The volume of the lake is 6 quadrillion gallons (23 quadrillion liters) and makes up to 80 percent of Russia's entire surface freshwater supply.

- The surface area of Baikal is 12,000 square miles (31,080 square kilometers), one-third of the surface area of North America's Lake Superior (31,800 square miles, or 82,362 square kilometers), but under the surface of Baikal are trenches able to swallow most of a 5,000-foot (1,524-meter) mountain turned upside down.

- Instead of a series of inlet and outlet rivers, the lake relies on a lopsided pattern: 336 rivers drain into the lake, but only the Angara River drains out.

- If all of the inlets and the one outlet to Baikal, the Angara River, were to be blocked, it would take 400 years for the basin to drain out through groundwater flow.

Source: Lake Baikal Basin, United Nations, 2002.

the water column feeding on algae. Able to reproduce every fifteen days, this endemic species, which numbers in the hundreds of millions, is a central food source for small fish.

Bird residents of the Baikal wetlands include the Siberian crane (*Grus leucogeranus*) and the Asian dowitcher (*Limnodromus semipalmatus*). Thriving in freshwater marshes, the dowitcher uses a distinct 5-inch-long (12.7-centimeter-long) bill to repeatedly probe into soft mud, consuming small clams, crustaceans, and aquatic worms.

Human Uses

Since the end of the last ice age, an estimated 14,000 years ago, humans have occupied the Lake Baikal region. Through hunting, fishing, and sowing and harvesting crops, hundreds of generations of residents have reaped the bountiful natural resources of this watershed. Prehistoric food processing areas, where fish were filleted and cooked or dried, have been found along the lakeshores over the years.

THE PEOPLE OF LAKE BAIKAL

- While ethnic Mongols settled in this area in the tenth century, Russians first arrived in this region in 1643, emigrating from the west and north.

- Thirty-five percent of the population is native Evenk and Buryat.

- There are thirty islands found within the lake, including Olkhon, the largest one (45 miles, or 73 kilometers, north to south and 9 miles, or 15 kilometers, east to west). Olkhon has 1,500 residents, in three towns. Most residents are employed in a fish factory.

- Native spiritual practices thrive here, including Tibetan Buddhism, Shamanism, and natural healing.

Ethnic Mongols called the Buryat settled on the eastern shores around 1000 C.E. They first named the lake *Baigal,* their word for "big reservoir." Today, this eastern region is part of Russia and is known as the Republic of Buryatia. Formed in 1923, the republic hosted a population of 981,238 as of 2008.

Located 45 miles (72 kilometers) west of the lake is the city of Irkutsk, settled in 1652 by Buryats who were seeking gold and an increase in their fur trading. The community became a government and business hub for the region known as Siberia. The Trans-Siberian Railway runs through this community of 593,600 residents living on the Angara River. Considered the cultural and artistic heart of the region after a number of artists were exiled here following a 1825 revolt, Irkutsk is colloquially termed the "Paris of Siberia." Due to limited access through primitive roadway systems, the majority of the northern lakeshore remains undeveloped and rural in character. In fact, winter passage on motorized vehicles across the frozen lake (called "zimink" in Russian, referring to the "frozen streets") is considered better than the majority of summer travel across the land. In all, about 150,000 people live in a dozen smaller farming communities along the lake region.

The economy of the Baikal basin is divided into distinct sectors: energy, industry, forestry, agriculture, fishing, and tourism. Approximately 29 percent of the economy relies on industrial work such as manufacturing, mining, and mineral processing. From land-based wells located throughout the region, 441,000 barrels of oil are pumped daily and exported for refining. Timber harvests provide 50 percent of Russia's pulp for paper products.

Up until 1990, when the Soviet Union collapsed, 1 million tourists visited Lake Baikal each year. Although this number has declined, a recent draw is eco-tourism, and an increasing number of international visitors come to the region.

There are considerable economic differences between the western side of the lake where Irkutsk is located and the eastern side of Buryatia. While Irkutsk residents have a more diversified and industrialized economy, earning up to $4,000 per capita, the Buryats have maintained their more agrarian roots and earn an average of $2,200 per year. Both regions rely on mineral wealth and exports of building materials, gas, gold, metals, oil, and salts.

Pollution and Damage

Russians warmly refer to Lake Baikal as "the pearl of the east" due to its considerable size and ecological diversity. Cultural stories and songs emphasize how soaking in the nutrient-rich waters provides healing properties.

Despite the lake's geographic isolation and small resident population, however, environmental impacts have accumulated, resulting in a reduction in water and air quality. In the last two decades, pollution has come from numerous point sources (fixed locations, such as mines and factories) and non-point sources (vary-ing locations, such as boats, motor vehicles, sewage, and storm water runoff).

The presence of a large paper and pulp mill, built in 1957 on the southern end of the lake in the town of Baikalsk, resulted in decades of water and air pollution. In a single day, this facility had the potential to produce tons of air-borne pollutants such as nitrous oxide and sulfur dioxide, as well as up to 13.2 million gallons (50 million liters) of liquid waste containing chlorine, phenols, dioxins, and other chemicals. The main product of the plant was a cellulose material commonly used in manufacturing. Wood pulp from this process was used in cloth and paper products and vehicle tires. Manufacturing 1 ton of pulp required 1.6 billion gallons (6 billion liters) of lake water. At its peak, the facility employed 4,500 workers from a town of 17,000. In 2008, the plant was shuttered due to reduced demands for wood products and poor pollution control practices. In early 2010, however, Russian Prime Minister Vladmir Putin ordered the plant reopened with technological improvements designed to better protect the lake.

In 2008, a fisherman shows his net encrusted with algae from Lake Baikal near the Baikalsk pulp and paper plant. Excessive algae blooms have been blamed on the plant's nutrient-rich chemical discharges, but the company that owns the mill says that the treated waste pumped into the lake is as safe to drink as the public water supplies in the capital city of Moscow. Another culprit for local water pollution is excessive nitrogen from untreated septic discharges along the southern Baikal shores. *(Bloomberg/Getty Images)*

KEY PROTECTED AREAS OF LAKE BAIKAL

Year Protected	Name	Location	Size (Square Miles)
1916	Barguzinskiy Zapovednik	Northeast	1,384
1969	Baikalskiy Zapovednik	South	639
1986	Baikalo-Lenskiy	West	2,548
1994	Selenga River Delta	Southeast	46
1995	Enkheluksky Reserve	Eastern	47
1999	Russian federal law passed to protect Lake Baikal	Entire coastal area	7,525

Source: *Lake Baikal Basin.* United Nations Environment Program, 2007.

The Selenga River flows into the southern section of Lake Baikal, and surface water runoff from industry, residential neighborhoods, and agricultural activities affects lake water quality. Despite the construction of up to 100 regional sewage treatment plants, raw human waste regularly flows into the lake, especially during heavy rains. The surrounding communities rely on coal-fired power and industrial plants, which are lightly regulated by the federal government. Mining debris from uplands often travels through wetlands and waterways, and cyanide and mercury are used to extract gold. Runoff flows through steep canyons to the Selenga, mixing with other elements, such as iron, chloride, and nitrogen. In addition, environmentalists have declared a uranium mine in nearby Khaigda to be a catastrophe due to its leakage of radioactive materials into the groundwater.

Researchers have performed numerous scientific studies examining a range of environmental issues in and around Lake Baikal. Mikhail Kozhov, a professor at a local university, began sampling conditions at a single location in the northwest region of the lake in 1945. The work was passed on to his daughter Olga Kozhova and granddaughter Lyubov Izmesteva.

More than sixty years of results prove that the lake is undergoing a number of complex changes. The water has increased in temperature by approximately 0.4 degrees Fahrenheit (0.7 degrees Celsius) every decade, and seasonal ice has formed on the lake approximately two weeks later each year. These changes have resulted in longer growing seasons for plankton and algae. Higher levels of nutrients, such as phosphorus and nitrogen, also have led to a tripling of chlorophyll (from the green pigment found in plants) levels, which is an indicator of declining water quality.

Despite the increased nutrients in the food chain, many coldwater species may not be able to adapt to temperature changes. The result, repeated elsewhere in a number of freshwater habitats, will be an ecological shift favoring plants and animals that thrive in warmer water. As of 2009, research on this project continues.

Mitigation and Management

Fed by as many as 336 separate surface water inlets and relying on only one outlet, Lake Baikal is susceptible to the buildup of pollutants. Although human population growth has been relatively slow, selected inputs such as sewer releases, mining deposits, agriculture runoff, and industrial pollution since the mid-twentieth century have accumulated in the waters and caused pollution. Future resource consumption and economic development could further impact the lake.

Local, state, and national governments have made progress in protecting large portions of land around the lake. In 1916, the first nature reserve, Barguzinskiy Zapovednik, was created along the northeast coastal region. Since then, a total of forty-five parks and nature reserves have been designated.

In 1987, the U.S.S.R. Council of Ministers declared a 21,814-square-mile (56,498-square-kilometer) Lake Baikal Coastal Protection Zone to limit forest activities on and near the lake. In 1994, the Ramsar Convention, an intergovernmental treaty that provides the framework for international conservation and the ethical use of wetlands, named the Selenga River Delta—one of the largest wetland systems in the world—a Ramsar Site of International Importance.

In 1996, the United Nations designated the lake as a World Heritage Site, noting, "Its age and isolation have produced one of the world's richest and most unusual freshwater faunas, which is of exceptional value to evolutionary science." This led to the protection of 11,969 square miles (31,000 square kilometers) of previously unprotected freshwater biomes.

In 1999, the Russian federal government passed the Baikal Law to regulate all economic and environmental activities in the Baikal watershed and to better address industrial and agricultural pollution in the area. In 2000, the Ministry of Natural Resources established a federal environmental protection agency, Baikalpriroda, to coordinate resource management.

Both local and international grassroots organizations have worked to conserve the lake. In 1990, Earth Island Institute, an environmental group based in San Francisco, created the Baikal Watch program to increase awareness of water quality and pollution issues. The Baikal Ecological Wave, based in the watershed, works with local citizens to expose pollution and illegal activity.

With limited roads or communities directly fronting the lake, increased ecotourism could improve economic conditions while simultaneously protecting the freshwater resources. Another goal is to construct a single recreational path, called the Great Baikal Trail, to circumnavigate the lakefront. Local and international groups built ninety-five segments by 2008, including 335 miles (539 kilometers) of new trails. Once completed, the trail system will span 1,120 miles (1,802 kilometers).

Under both local and international pressure, the Russian government re-routed a planned oil pipeline away from the northern shore of Lake Baikal in 2006. As originally planned, this $11.5 billion, 2,500-mile (4,023-kilometer) pipeline would have run within 0.5 miles (0.8 kilometers) of the lake. Government, environmental, scientific, and other groups recognized the risk of oil spillage from this project as too great—rupture of the line would send oil gushing downhill into the freshwater ecosystem. The pipeline subsequently was repositioned 25 miles (40 kilometers) away from Baikal.

One of the biggest challenges for the future of Lake Baikal is coordination among government officials, scientists, and nonprofit agencies representing the Russian states surrounding the watershed. Environmental funding has declined since the early 1990s, resulting in a reduced ability for those seeking to protect and preserve Lake Baikal to draft watershed management plans, restore damaged areas, and monitor overall freshwater quality.

Selected Web Sites

Baikal Watch: http://www.earthisland.org/baikal/.
The Great Baikal Trail: http://www.greatbaikaltrail.org/index_en.html.
Lake Baikal, United Nations World Heritage Site: http://whc.unesco.org/en/list/754.
Lake Baikal Case Study: http://www.american.edu/TED/baikal.htm.
Lake Baikal Map, National Geographic: http://www.irkutsk.org/baikal/ng/ng.jpg.
Tahoe-Baikal Institute: http://www.tahoebaikal.org.

Further Reading

Matthiessen, Peter. *Baikal: Sacred Sea of Siberia.* New York: Random House, 1992.
Minoura, Koji, ed. *Lake Baikal: A Mirror in Time and Space for Understanding Global Change Processes.* Amsterdam, The Netherlands: Elsevier Science, 2000.
Tahoe-Baikal Institute. *Baikal Reader.* South Lake Tahoe, CA: Tahoe-Baikal Institute, 2004.
Thompson, Peter. *Sacred Sea: A Journey to Lake Baikal.* New York: Oxford University Press, 2007.

United Nations. *Lake Baikal Basin–Russian Federation*. Cambridge, UK: United Nations Protected Areas Program, 2002.

Venable, Sondra. *Protecting Lake Baikal*. Saarbrücken, Germany: VDM Verlag, 2008.

6 Kuwait
Middle East

The nation of Kuwait contains almost no measurable surface freshwater due to the influence of the Arabian Desert and its overwhelmingly arid climate. This poses a distinct challenge for a resident population that must derive freshwater for daily needs.

Located in the western Middle East at the northern edge of the Persian Gulf on the Arabian Peninsula, this independent Arab Emirate contains 6,880 square miles (17,819 square kilometers) of land. It fronts the saltwater gulf on its eastern boundary and is bordered by the much larger countries of Iraq to the north and west and Saudi Arabia to the south. At 120 miles (193 kilometers) north to south and 170 miles (274 kilometers) west to east, Kuwait is one of the world's smallest countries (about the size of the state of Connecticut) and one of the wealthiest due to the presence of considerable oil and natural gas deposits.

The Arabian Desert stretches across both the Saudi Arabian Peninsula and the Persian Gulf region. The highest point in Kuwait is 922 feet (281 meters) on its western boundary. Parts of the desert terrain are similar to a moonscape. Sun-driven winds pile sand into dunes that stretch for miles and are devoid of streams, rivers, or ponds.

In the summer months, searing temperatures exceed 120 degrees Fahrenheit (49 degrees Celsius), and this influences the formation of violent sandstorms. In the limited rainy season, from October to May, precipitation rarely surpasses 4 inches (10 centimeters) per year. Although rain may result in temporary surface water during the cooler winters, when temperatures can drop as low as 45

KUWAIT REPTILES

Common Name	Scientific Name	Characteristics
Arabian Sand Boa	*Eryx jayakari*	This toothless species winds around its prey and squeezes it to death before swallowing it whole.
Black Desert Cobra	*Walterinnesia aegyptica*	This snake commonly eats the spiny-tailed lizard, forcing its way into the lizard's den and then biting and paralyzing the lizard with the powerful neurotoxin in its venom.
Monitor Lizard	*Varanus griseus sp.*	This lizard's name, translated from the Arabian word *waral* meaning "monitor," refers to the creature's habit of standing on its two rear legs to scan the horizon.
Spiny-tailed Lizard	*Uromastyx sp.*	Up to fifteen different species of these lizards inhabit the Arabian Desert; most have spiked ridges that provide a good defense against predators.

degrees Fahrenheit (7 degrees Celsius) during the night, little water seeps down underground; instead, it is rapidly evaporated by the dry winds.

Plants and animals living in the Arabian Desert must adapt to withstand hyperarid conditions brought on by intense sunlight, searing heat, and a lack of rain. When the seasonal rains arrive, up to 400 species of grasses and flowering plants suddenly flourish. These include al awsaj (*Lycium Arbicum*), a small plant with thorny leaves that draws insects from miles away with its bright red flowers. Another plant, arfaj (*Phanterium epapposum*), is a common, low-growing grass favored by browsing camels.

Animals that survive in these harsh conditions include the sand cat (*Felis margarita harrisoni*), a dark yellow feline that lives in rocky areas and only hunts in the cooler nighttime. At 20 inches (51 centimeters) long by 12 inches (30 centimeters) tall, this 5-pound (2.3-kilogram) cat has a wide head and ears that allow it to hear the movement of prey such as insects and lizards across distances.

There are thirty-eight reptile species in the Kuwait region. Reptiles that thrive in the desert include the frog-eyed gecko (*Teratoscincus scincus*). This gecko prefers the coastal plains where its orange-, yellow-, and black-spotted body blends into the dune terrain. The gecko digs a burrow up to 4 feet (1.2 meters) deep, creating a home that is cooler and more humid than its surrounding conditions. Known for a wide-ranging diet that includes other lizards and insects, it relies on rapid movements and noteworthy "barks" to scare away other predators in the night.

Human Uses

Modern settlement in the Persian Gulf region dates back to 1613, when small groups of central Asians migrated from drought-stricken areas west to more lush eastern Arabian communities. In 1705, one of the stronger tribes, named the Bani Utbah, formed a government and named the community Guraine. One of the most desirable features of the settlement was its deepwater harbor. Later named Kuwait, the growing port town relied on trade between Africa, India, and the Middle East. Shipbuilding and domestic products, such as pearls, dried fish, dates, and spices, fueled the economy.

In the 1890s, Kuwait used an agreement with Great Britain to keep the Ottoman Empire (Turkey) from occupying the harbor and taxing its shipping traffic. Further treaties with Great Britain resulted in that nation's control over Kuwaiti foreign policy and national security. In the 1930s, the discovery of oil fields rapidly transformed the region. After having agreements and conventions with both the Ottoman and British empires, Kuwait declared its independence in 1961. Today, it is ruled as a constitutional monarchy by an emir and a national

KUWAIT'S OIL–BASED ECONOMY

- Oil sales account for 80 percent of total economic earnings and 95 percent of the exports.

- Although oil fields have been heavily pumped, up to 101 billion barrels remain, nearly 9 percent of the global reserves.

- The per capita income of $38,876 in 2009 ranked the nation as the eleventh richest in the world.

- The oil-generated economic growth has supported a population boom, with a growth rate up to 3.5 percent annually; up to 48 percent of the population is under the age of twenty-five.

Source: Government of Kuwait.

assembly. Unprecedented growth in oil extraction has resulted in an annual economy worth upwards of $138 billion.

Kuwait's population of 3.3 million residents is centered in urban areas, such as Kuwait City, which has 1.4 million residents. Massive construction projects have caused Kuwait to employ considerable numbers of foreign workers from countries such as India, Pakistan, and the Philippines; approximately 63 percent of the country's residents are not citizens.

Less than 3 percent of the population lives in rural areas due to the lack of water and power. Across the country, less than 300 square miles (777 square kilometers) of land currently is farmed, mostly due to limited usable wells, high water costs, and steep grain costs for livestock, such as cattle. Like an island, Kuwait relies mostly on food imported from around the world to feed its people.

In order to provide freshwater, wells were dug in community centers as far back as the 1720s, tapping into groundwater aquifers in sedimentary rock beds. These supplies, some of which had sat untouched for up to 400,000 years, had been fed slowly over time by the lateral movement of freshwater through layers of porous stone.

The first country to adopt seawater desalination to compensate for a severe lack of quality freshwater supplies, Kuwait has coupled its filtering process with electricity generation. Steam created from the generation of electricity is harnessed for power to drive the desalination process. *(Three Lions/Stringer/Getty Images)*

Groundwater, however, does not have sufficient recharge from rainwater in the desert environment. Due to a buildup of salts and sediment, wells often are rapidly depleted or become nonpotable (salinity above 1,000 parts per million).

The government of Kuwait has had to rely on alternative sources of freshwater. Between 1925 and 1950, imported water from Iraq supplemented groundwater wells that were laced with salts from the Persian Gulf. It was not until the late 1940s that the government began to develop a public water supply system. By 1950, the first desalination plant, located in Kuwait City, was brought online to treat well water.

Utilizing a process called "multi-stage flashing," desalination turns salt water into freshwater by rapidly heating the salt water several times. The resulting freshwater steam is captured and separated from accumulated sediment and salts. Desalination facilities, which are costly to run because their numerous pumps require a large amount of electricity, are able to reduce the dissolved salt content from as high as 45,000 parts per million to 25 to 50 parts per million.

In the 1980s, two more large desalination plants near Kuwait City were completed, one utilizing brackish groundwater and the other using gulf water. By 2008, a total of eight plants were in use; 59 percent of water resources came from desalination, 32 percent from groundwater wells, and 9 percent from wastewater reuse.

Pollution and Damage

Arid countries such as Kuwait can face severe social and economic hardships due to a lack of freshwater. Groundwater wells across Kuwait suffer from two simultaneous fates: overpumping and salt or sediment invasion.

In 1991, almost half of the country's freshwater came from wells. By 2002, that number had been reduced to 32 percent, and it is expected to continue shrinking. Estimates for the total natural inflow of freshwater into the two major aquifers is less than 5.3 billion gallons (20 billion liters) per year, all of it sourced from Saudi Arabia. Up to half of all wells in the south and up to 55 percent of those in the north have a salinity level in excess of 7,500 parts per million.

Another problem is that the process of desalination applies considerable pressure to the adjacent coastal environment. When freshwater is separated from salt water, the wastewater product is an extremely salty solution. Dumped back into local gulf waters, this briny mixture harms the marine environment by changing the water's salt concentration, temperature, and turbidity (cloudiness of a fluid caused by suspended sediments).

Many bird and fish species cannot survive in these conditions, although algae, some mollusks, and nematodes can live in this extreme environment. Efforts to reduce impacts from desalination plants have included diluting effluent, building outfall pipes farther underwater offshore, and reducing the volume rate of discharge into waterways.

Although economically successful, Kuwaiti oil wells have caused disputes with neighboring Iraq. Following a long-term border dispute, a drop in oil prices, and accusations of oil removal from its neighboring Rumaila fields in southern Iraq, the Iraqi army invaded Kuwait in August 1990. A coalition of thirty-four countries led by the United States executed a large military campaign in 1991 to repel and disable the Iraqi army.

When Iraqi troops fled from Kuwait in 1991, Iraqi soldiers set fire to 789 oil wells. Enormous fires raged for weeks, and millions of gallons of oil spilled across the land, into groundwater supplies, and into the Persian Gulf. Two hundred and forty separate oil lakes were documented across the desert. In March 1991, the fires consumed 6 million barrels of oil each day, producing enough floating black soot to cover an area half the size of the United States.

One of the biggest impacts of the oil spills was the crude oil that drained from well fields into groundwater supplies and the Persian Gulf. An estimated 250 million gallons (946 million liters), twenty times the amount from the 1989 *Exxon Valdez* oil tanker spill in Alaska, were visible, covering 440 miles (708 kilometers) of coastline. Due to the weak currents at the northern reaches of the gulf, it will take decades for bacteria and the movement of water to break down the oil.

On land, international sources estimated that 1 billion barrels of oil soaked into underground aquifers. Sinking under the surface, oil leaches into groundwater, prohibiting human consumption for decades. By 2007, Kuwait had spent up to $8 billion to repair oil wells and clean up spills, but reaching deep aquifers is a very slow and expensive process and, due to the low population nearby, not considered a high priority compared to coastal salt water clean up efforts.

Mitigation and Management

One of Kuwait's biggest challenges is getting a sufficient amount of water to its residents and businesses. In 2001, Kuwait and Iran unveiled plans to build a 313-mile-long (504-kilometer-long) freshwater pipeline, which would carry water from the Karkheh Dam in western Iran to Kuwait. Although the proposed $2 billion pipeline would deliver up to 52 million gallons (197 million liters) of water per day into Kuwait, its expense and potential to diminish Iran's domestic supplies of freshwater have slowed progress on the project.

In response, the Kuwaiti government has invested up to $500 million to develop state-of-the-art, large-volume water delivery systems within Kuwait, including a desalination plant that uses filters and reverse osmosis (a method of filtration where water is pushed through a membrane to remove particles and certain chemicals) to treat salty gulf waters. The plant is designed to provide 3.5 million gallons (13 million liters) of freshwater per day, which is enough for 450,000 residents. In addition, by using filtration technology with very fine porous membranes, it saves up to $7.2 million per year in operating costs. The new plant began filtration in 2010.

In the meantime, the technology necessary to provide publicly supplied water across Kuwait continues to improve and become more efficient. Kuwait has built cogeneration facilities in which the waste heat from electricity-generating plants is recaptured and used in desalination steps, cutting energy needs in half.

In 2008, the Kuwait Institute for Scientific Research, an independent public institution that conducts scientific and applied research to preserve the environment and advise the government of scientific issues, released a report recommending that the government increase its water storage abilities in order to

KUWAIT WATER DEMANDS

A number of short- and long-term freshwater challenges exist:

- The population continues to grow at a rate of more than 2.4 percent per year, according to 2008 World Bank statistics.

- Daily demand for freshwater in 2007 was in excess of 619 million gallons (2.3 billion liters), according to the Kuwait University Engineering Department.

- Daily water consumption in 1954 was 76.5 million gallons (290 million liters) per day and by 2020, demand is expected to exceed 1 billion gallons (3.8 billion liters) a day.

- Year-round demand for water has resulted in the government water utility implementing a number of conservation measures, including launching an educational campaign on how to save water, establishing higher costs for water use, and requiring that new buildings are fitted with water-efficient fixtures.

hold up to a year's worth of public water. A growing population and escalating costs to obtain freshwater connect water security to economic health. While the Kuwaiti government has spent $344 million since the late 1990s to build large metal storage tanks and underground concrete reservoirs, the institute concluded that natural subterranean aquifers could provide the same water storage capacity at roughly 5 percent of the cost of man-made structures. This approach has been used successfully elsewhere in the region.

Selected Web Sites

Kuwait Institute for Scientific Research: http://www.waterkuwait.com.

Government of Kuwait, Ministry of Energy, History of Water System: http://www.mew.gov.kw/Default.aspx?pageId=505.

Kuwait Water Profile by United Nations Food and Agriculture Organization: http://www.fao.org/nr/water/aquastat/countries/kuwait/index.stm.

Kuwait Water Resources (from Kuwait Ministry of Information): http://www.kuwait-info.com/a_state_of_kuwait/state_kuwait_gwater.asp.

Further Reading

Allan, Tony. *The Middle East Water Question*. New York: I.B. Tauris, 2002.

Casey, Michael S. *The History of Kuwait*. Portsmouth, NH: Greenwood, 2007.

Fadlelmawla, Amr, et al. *Analysis of the Water Resources Status in Kuwait*. Dordrecht, The Netherlands: Springer, Water Resources Management, 2005.

Kuwait Institute for Scientific Research. *Food Security and Strategic Water Reserves in Kuwait*. Safat, Kuwait: Kuwait Institute for Scientific Research, 2008.

7 New York City New York

The biggest city in the United States relies on one of the largest public fresh-water supply systems in the world. With 8.3 million residents spread across five boroughs, New York City is an international megalopolis that occupies 304 square miles (787 square kilometers). Population density across the landscape of multi-story buildings and skyscrapers exceeds 27,440 residents per square mile.

New York City has only a limited ability to provide some freshwater from local sources, such as groundwater wells, to certain neighborhoods. To quench the majority of the city's thirst, it has built an impressive freshwater delivery system over the course of two centuries. The system utilizes nineteen reservoirs on 1,972 square miles (5,107 square kilometers) of protected land located as far as 125 miles (201 kilometers) from the city itself. This network, which supplies up to 1 billion gallons (3.8 billion liters) of freshwater every day, has won extensive awards and recognition for the purity and taste of the water provided.

Located in the northern Mid-Atlantic region at the edge of the Atlantic Ocean, New York City sits at the intersection of three states, New York, New Jersey, and Connecticut. Its position at the mouth of the Hudson River, where the river flows into the ocean, marks a region where freshwater and salt water mix.

The city's five boroughs—the Bronx, Brooklyn, Manhattan, Queens, and Staten Island—are spread across a portion of land attached to the New York State mainland, a cluster of three prominent islands (Staten Island, Manhattan, and a segment of Long Island), as well as several smaller ones. The city is flanked by three water bodies: on the west by the Hudson River, on the east by Long Island Sound (which is part of the Atlantic Ocean), and on the south by the open ocean.

NEW YORK CITY WATER SUPPLY SYSTEM

Watershed System/ Reservoir Name	Water Capacity (Billions of Gallons)
Catskill and Delaware Watersheds	
Ashokan	122
Cannonsville	95
Neversink	34
Pepacton	140
Rondout	49
Schoharie	17
Croton System	
Amawalk	6.7
Bog Brook	4.4
Boyds Corner	1.7
Cross River	10.3
Croton Falls	14.2
East Branch	5.2
Kensico	30.6
Middle Branch	4.1
Muscoot	4.9
New Croton	19
West Branch	8
Total:	566

Source: New York City Department of Environmental Protection, 2008.

The city is built on a natural foundation of bedrock and glacially deposited outwash, most of which sits just 10 to 20 feet (3 and 6 meters) above sea level. Much of the city's landscape, however, has been changed by the deposition of fill, applied in most cases to elevate areas that held wetlands or lands that periodically flooded.

The city's weather can be highly variable due to its location at the intersection of land and water. The open ocean makes temperatures more moderate than nearby inland locations, making it somewhat cooler in summer and warmer in winter. Summers can be hot and humid, with July temperatures reaching an average high of 84 degrees Fahrenheit (29 degrees Celsius) and average low of 76 degrees Fahrenheit (24 degrees Celsius). Although winds can be very strong in midwinter, the average winter high temperature is 43 degrees Fahrenheit (6 degrees Celsius) and average low is 31 degrees Fahrenheit (-0.6 degrees Celsius).

Annual precipitation averages approximately 46 inches (117 centimeters). This may include up to 25 inches (64 centimeters) of snow, though most does not stay frozen for long on city streets and sidewalks.

Human Uses

When the Italian explorer Giovanni da Verrazano discovered the land that would become New York City in 1524, it was a pristine landscape occupied by small groups of Delaware or Lenni Lenape Indians. His ship navigated to an area off Staten Island, where a landing crew went ashore to gather a precious resource for explorers: freshwater.

By 1626, the Dutch had acquired what is today Manhattan after trading with the native peoples. In 1664, the British took possession of the area, renaming it after the Duke of York. This coastal community was flourishing when New York City's

The Jaqueline Kennedy Onassis Reservoir, also known as the Central Park Reservoir, is a 106-acre (43-hectare) freshwater reservoir that holds up to 1 billion gallons (3.8 billion liters) of water. Beginning in 1862, this body of water was used as a collecting point for Manhattan's freshwater distribution system. It was replaced in 1993 by a newer network of large underground pipes. (© John Anderson/Fotolia)

first public well was dug in 1677 at Bowling Green in the south end of Manhattan. Even at this early point in the city's history, a major issue became apparent: the difficulty of obtaining good quality freshwater. Much of this problem had to do with the low-lying land, dense bedrock, and salt water on three sides.

As the population swelled to 25,000 at the turn of the nineteenth century, its water challenges also increased. The city formed a private corporation in 1799 to address the groundwater supply and pollution problems. Relying at first on shallow groundwater wells and a primitive system of wooden pipes, the Manhattan Company (now the Chase Manhattan Bank) spent the bare minimum to provide community wells.

KEY FRESHWATER EVENTS FOR NEW YORK CITY

1832: Up to 3,516 residents die in a single outbreak of cholera.

1842: The Croton Reservoir, built at a cost of $12 million, begins flowing to the city, peaking at 90 million gallons (341 million liters) per day.

1915: The first segment of what will become known as the Catskill System is completed with the construction of the Ashokan Reservoir and the Catskill Aqueduct.

1928–1931: An approved expansion in 1928 to acquire water from the upper Delaware River is challenged by the state of New Jersey, but the U.S. Supreme Court upholds the project in 1931.

1970: Tunnel Number 3, a 60-mile-long (97-kilometer-long) transport pipe that spans up to 43 feet (13.1 meters) in diameter, is begun. It is expected to be completed in 2020, and the estimated total cost of this construction project is $6 billion.

2007: Proving the quality of the water system, the federal government establishes a 10-year regulatory waiver of filtering requirements for water from upstate because of its natural clarity. Up to 90 percent of the city water originates in the Catskill-Delaware area.

Source: New York City Department of Environmental Protection, 2008.

For the next thirty-three years, New Yorkers were left with an insufficient system of basic groundwater wells. The groundwater also was polluted by raw human and animal sewage and posed a public health threat. This condition resulted in the spread of epidemic diseases such as cholera. In 1832, government leaders deemed the private water supply contract to be a failure and stepped in to implement a plan to supply clean water, which included identifying water supplies outside the city.

Two years later, the city began buying land in Westchester County, approximately 20 miles (32 kilometers) to the north. By the 1840s, it had constructed reservoirs and an aqueduct to deliver water to the downtown area. Other reservoirs were built in Westchester, with a second aqueduct put in service in 1890.

By the turn of the twentieth century, the city population had reached 3.4 million and was growing rapidly. With limited water and land resources in the area, the city officials opted to look west and north, to the Catskill Mountains. Securing support from Catskill residents and the state in 1905, the city began to develop the Catskill System. Originally consisting of one large reservoir and about 20,000 acres (8,094 hectares) of land, it provided freshwater to the city within a decade.

By 1920, the city's population had almost doubled since 1900 to nearly 6 million residents, and water demands had grown considerably. The city received approval to use the upper Delaware River, to the west of the Catskill watershed, for its next injection of water in 1931. Construction of the Delaware System began in 1937, and the Delaware Aqueduct and four new reservoirs were in service by 1964. By 2007, the entire Catskill-Delaware reservoir system included 1,972 square miles (5,107 square kilometers) of undeveloped land surrounding nineteen reservoirs with a storage capacity of 580 billion gallons (2,196 billion liters) of water.

Modern New York City has become a powerhouse in the entertainment, financial services, and tourism sectors, as well as a center for international government and business relations. It hosts financial centers such as Wall Street and headquarters of international organizations such as the United Nations. Visitors flock to the Broadway theater district, Times Square, the Statue of Liberty, world-renowned museums, and entertainment and sporting events.

Residents are employed in a spectrum of jobs, led by business professionals in the financial services, government, legal, and medical fields. A considerable service sector—including the food service industry, educators, public safety personnel, and transportation systems—also plays a critical role in supporting the daily needs of the city.

The average salary among 3.7 million full-time employees was $50,820 in 2007. Given the desirability of living in Manhattan, prices for homes have soared. In 2009, the average apartment sale price in this borough was $1.39 million.

Pollution and Damage

Although upstate water sources benefited city residents with safe, clean water, the removal of more than 1 billion gallons (3.8 billion liters) of water per day from several watersheds in Westchester County and the Catskill Mountains has impacted the ecology and hydrology of these natural areas by reducing water levels across multiple rivers and streams. The construction of reservoirs has resulted in the submergence of thousands of acres of land, resulting in the loss of forest and wetland habitats. In this process, several thousand residents were relocated, and buildings and graveyards were moved.

New York City's upstate reservoirs and water systems also have created a zone of enforced preservation around the water sources. This has had the effect of increasing scrutiny of any form of economic development in local communities in favor of protecting the city's water supply.

After years of claiming crystal-clear waters that required little filtration, New York City has been challenged by incidents of sediment-filled water. This condition, also called turbidity, occurs when storms and the resulting runoff dump sand and dirt into the water, often making it cloudy and tinged with a light brown color. One intense storm in 2005 washed construction site materials into reservoirs, prompting health officials to issue an order for city residents to boil their water.

Runoff often contains naturally occurring microscopic organisms such as cryptosporidium and giardia, which can flourish in unfiltered water and threaten humans with intestinal illnesses. The first step taken by city water managers was to use more chlorine to sanitize the water. During the 1990s, the city implemented a 35 percent increase in chlorine use. The next approach was to use the chemical aluminum sulfate (commonly called alum) in particulate form to clear the water. When broadcast into reservoirs, sediment binds to the material, and it settles to the bottom of the water body, resulting in clearer water. While these procedures may have worked on a few occasions, they are not long-term solutions and have been criticized by the U.S. Environmental Protection Agency (EPA) and the New York State attorney general.

In 1998, city officials agreed to build a $1 billion plant to begin treating the water of the Croton Reservoirs to increase water quality and comply with state and federal laws; this project is expected to start in 2011. In 2007, New York City was able to obtain a substantial waiver of federal water quality filtration requirements due to its high-quality water. This exemption from the EPA delayed the construction of an $8 billion filtration plant for water from the Catskills and Delaware watersheds for at least ten years, until the water quality is reviewed again.

Mitigation and Management

New York City's accomplishment of building a water system able to supply more than 8.3 million residents with sufficient and high-quality freshwater is impressive. To assemble a similar system today, especially under strict environmental reviews and with the current cost of land, would be financially prohibitive and most likely would be fiercely resisted by local communities.

On the right is a slice of wooden pipe from the original New York City water distribution system, built from bored-out elm logs. Laid around 1867 by the Manhattan Company (a private company hired by the city to install and maintain the public water system), this wooden pipe was unearthed during the construction of a new tunnel. Shown above is the first portion of Tunnel Number 3, which went into service in 1998; this tunnel still is under construction and is not expected to be completed until 2020. *(New York Daily News/Getty Images)*

UPSTATE WATER SUPPLY

The city is required to provide public water to towns and cities near the Croton and Catskill reservoirs. By the numbers, this includes:

- Eight upstate counties.

- Sixty municipal connections.

- Up to 120 million gallons (454 million liters) per day.

- Providing water for 1 million New York State residents outside New York City.

Source: New York City Department of Environmental Protection, 2008.

In order to keep the city's freshwater delivery system in top condition, major renovation work and new construction are performed on a regular basis. The biggest project—the approximately $6 billion construction of Tunnel Number 3, a structure measuring up to 43 feet (13.1 meters) in diameter and sitting up to 800 feet (244 meters) below ground—includes 60 miles (97 kilometers) of piping in three stages between Manhattan and the city of Yonkers, to the north. This tunnel is being built to allow for work on the 1917 and 1936 tunnels, which have never been taken out of service and fully inspected since they were built. Although the two original tunnels have been reliable, the New York City Department of Environmental Protection estimates that up to one-quarter of all water (up to 36 million gallons a day) traveling through them may leak out at some point. Started in 1970, work on Tunnel Number 3 is slated to be completed in 2020.

New York City has employed a watershed protection program to guarantee that its freshwater system stays clean and is properly managed for future generations. This includes a number of efforts at and around the reservoir sites.

Repair of old and leaking septic systems on privately owned property in the Catskill Mountains is a priority. This is because such systems can send, through the movement of groundwater, untreated human waste into the watershed and, eventually, the water supply. Between 1997 and 2008, the city paid $28.6 million to repair or replace over 1,000 private septic systems. Funds also are expended to pay for regular septic system pumping to maintain disposal systems and reduce leaching into adjacent watersheds.

Another program involves storm water management around the Catskill reservoirs. When heavy rains flow across pavement and saturated soils, they can push debris such as oil, animal waste, fertilizer, and other contaminants into the reservoirs. Attempting to control this "first flush," the city invested $7.6 million in 1997 and $7.5 million in 2003 to build better screens and other storm water treatment devices in order to filter and treat this water before it arrives at the public water supply. Projects include new catch basins with several layers of filtration to prevent direct discharge into water bodies.

Although the city grew in population from 7.1 million people in 1979 to 8.3 million in 2009, freshwater use decreased 28 percent during this time. One reason was the implementation of broad regulatory requirements, including lower-use toilets and faucet fixtures, especially for new buildings and renovations.

Another measure involved locating and repairing water leaks, both above and below ground. A third effort, possibly lowering water usage the most, was the installation of water meters at all residential and business locations and the imposition of water rates that better reflect capital costs.

Selected Web Sites

New York City Department of Environmental Protection: http://nyc.gov/html/dep.

The New York City Water Story, American Museum of Natural History: http://www.amnh.org/education/resources/rfl/web/nycwater/.

New York City Water Tunnel Number 3 Factsheet: http://www.nyc.gov/html/dep/pdf/factsheet.pdf.

Further Reading

Bone, Kevin, ed. *Water-Works: The Architecture and Engineering of the New York City Water Supply System.* New York: Monacelli, 2006.

Galusha, Diana. *Liquid Assets.* Fleischmanns, NY: Purple Mountain, 2002.

Greenberg, Stanley. *Waterworks.* New York: Princeton Architectural Press, 2003.

Hall, Edward Hagaman. *The Catskill Aqueduct and Earlier Water Supplies of the City of New York.* 1917. Ann Arbor: University of Michigan, 2006.

Koeppel, Gerard T. *Water for Gotham: A History.* Princeton, NJ: Princeton University Press, 2000.

McCully, Betsy. *City at the Water's Edge.* Piscataway, NJ: Rutgers University Press, 2007.

Tompkins, Christopher R. *The Croton Dams and Aqueduct.* Charleston, SC: Acadia, 2000.

8 Murray-Darling Basin Australia

One of Australia's most significant agricultural regions, the Murray-Darling Basin spans 386,102 square miles (100,004 square kilometers) across the southeastern continent, or approximately 14 percent of the landmass. The size of Spain and France combined, the basin crosses four states, including all of the Australian Capital Territory, 75 percent of New South Wales, 15 percent of Queensland, and 8 percent of South Australia.

The basin's two major water bodies are the Murray and Darling rivers, which together contain 6 percent of Australia's freshwater resources. Up to 2 million people live in this basin; another 1 million rely on the freshwater from the region for daily needs. In addition, regional agriculture utilizes extensive irrigation systems. Farms across the area, consisting of both cropland and rangeland, generate 40 percent of Australia's annual agricultural output.

Spanning a diversity of landscapes that include humid eastern uplands, semi-arid western plains, and subtropical northern lands, this region is known for its mostly arid terrain. A growing population, approximately 2 percent per year, and severe droughts in southeastern Australia in the last three decades have resulted in a lack of freshwater supplies, posing complex environmental, social, and economic challenges for the nation as a whole.

The Murray River is Australia's longest river, flowing 1,608 miles (2,587 kilometers) from east to west between the states of New South Wales and Victoria. The Murray originates in the Australian Alps, including its highest peak, Mount Kosciuszko (7,310 feet, or 2,228 meters). Combined freshwater mountain runoff

The red-tailed black cockatoo (*Calyptorhynchus banksii*) is a highly intelligent and adaptable regional species that often lives in hollowed-out tree cavities. This cockatoo species, which forages in flocks for a diet rich in nuts and seeds, is threatened in the southern part of Australia, due to the combination of lost forest and wetland habitats related to the effects of a long-term drought. (*© Rok Venturini/ Fotolia*)

can exceed 27,100 cubic feet (767 cubic meters) per second in the middle of the spring snowmelt. The terminus of the river, the Southern Ocean, consists of a relatively narrow mouth with only a small estuary, due to the fact that much of the water has been consumed or has evaporated by the time it reaches the coast.

One common species in this river is the Murray cod (*Maccullochella peelii peelii*), an endemic fish that reaches 40 inches (102 centimeters) in length and 215 pounds (98 kilograms) in weight. This species of freshwater cod lays eggs on surfaces such as exposed rock beds and submerged logs. Its diet consists of smaller fish, including carp, catfish, perch, and smelt.

The Darling River is Australia's third-longest river, at 863 miles (1,389 kilometers) long. It runs from New South Wales in the eastern foothills of the Great Dividing Range and travels toward the Murray River in a southwestern direction. At the town of Wentworth, the Darling River drains into the Murray River. The Darling River's watershed is 42,915 square miles (111,150 square kilometers), approximately 15 percent of the size of the Murray. Known for its shallow waters, it transverses a mostly flat terrain (in some sections, the elevation only descends an average of 1 inch to the mile, or 2.54 centimeters to the kilometer). Although the eastern portion of the river receives up to 16 inches (41 centimeters) of rain per year, the western section is much drier, receiving only 6 inches (15 centimeters).

The flow of the Darling River is irregular; between 1885 and 1960, it dried up forty-five times during the summer months. On average, the river loses up to 94 percent of its flow due to evaporation in arid conditions. Its current state is classified as "overdeveloped" in the Australian Natural Resource Atlas due to excessive water withdrawals (up to 39 percent is removed for farmland irrigation), a high salt concentration, and pollution from agricultural pesticide runoff.

Despite these challenges, the area is rich in wildlife, hosting 367 bird species, eighty-five mammal species, 100 lizard species, fifty-three frog species, forty-six snake species, and thirty-four fish species. Unique birds, such as the red-tailed black cockatoo (*Calyptorhynchus banksii samueli*), live along its banks and floodplains. Living in eucalyptus woodlands, the cockatoo nests in the hollowed-out cavities of large trees. Although not a migrating species, these gregarious birds move around seasonally in search of food such as young plants, fruits, nuts, and seeds.

History

The modern geologic history of southeastern Australia stretches back to 65 million years ago, when a large section of land broke off from the continent of Antarctica. Moving to the north, this new continent featured a saucer-like depression in its southeastern portion. Up to 269 miles (433 kilometers) in diameter and 1,968 feet (600 meters) deep in its center, this region experienced very warm weather, supporting abundant tropical rain forests. Rising sea levels caused an inland sea to cover much of the Murray-Darling Basin 20 million years ago; these waters eventually retreated 12 million years ago. Remaining sand and salt formed multiple layers in the soils.

A large inland freshwater body, Lake Bungunnia, developed some 2 million years ago, when a natural dam formed at its lower reaches. The lake spanned 11,583 square miles (30,000 square kilometers), or roughly the size of Lake Erie, one of North America's Great Lakes and the thirteenth-largest lake in the world. By 700,000 years ago, the lake drained when the dam eroded away, and the climate became more arid. Despite 20 million years of deposition of rocks, minerals, and organic material into the basin, it remains mostly flat, with the highest elevation being 660 feet (201 meters) above sea level.

Human Uses

Aboriginal peoples lived in southeastern Australia as far back as 40,000 years ago. Proof of human settlements along the Murray River came from radiocarbon dating of a large cache of buried freshwater mussel (*Mycetopus rugatus*) shells, which were well preserved in the low-oxygen mud of the riverbank.

When explorers from England first arrived in southeastern Australia in 1824, they found a semi-arid landscape that was undeveloped and only occupied by a few groups of native peoples. By 1840, settlers had claimed large sections of land

NATIVE STORY OF THE RIVER

One Aboriginal Ngarrindjeri story, passed on for thousands of years, documents a dream about the basin and how the rivers were shaped:

In the dreaming, Ngurunderi (a hero) traveled down the River Murray in a bark canoe, in search of his two wives who had run away from him. At the time, the River was only a small stream below the junction with the Darling River.

Ponde (a giant cod fish) swam ahead of Ngurunderi, widening the river with sweeps of its tail. Ngurunderi chased the fish, trying to spear it from his canoe. Near Murray Bridge, he threw his spear but it missed and became Long Island. At Tailem Bend, he threw another; the giant fish surged ahead and created a long straight stretch in the River.

At last, at last, with the help of Nepele (the brother of Ngurunderi's wives), Ponde was speared after it had left the River Murray and had swam into Lake Alexandrina. Ngurunderi divided the fish with his stone knife and created a new species of fish from each piece.

Source: Ngurunderi: An Aboriginal Dreaming. Adelaide, Australia: South Australian Museum, 2009.

adjacent to the Murray River, irrigating their crops with nearby water. By 1853, two large paddleboats were making trips up and down the basin, turning the rivers into an inland highway. However, river transportation declined after 1883, when newly laid rail lines provided the capacity for year-round locomotive transport of people and goods.

The River Murray Waters Agreement of 1915, signed between the state governments of New South Wales, South Australia, and Victoria, set conditions to divide water withdrawals among multiple stakeholders. By 1979, four large reservoirs, sixteen weirs, and five barrages controlled significant portions of the natural flow of the Murray River.

In 2008, there were 61,033 farms located within the basin, generating up to 39 percent of Australia's agricultural products, valued at $15 billion a year. Approximately 43 percent of the farms host livestock pasture, 20 percent grow grains, 15 percent produce cotton, 6 percent grow rice, 6 percent cultivate grapes, 5 percent grow nuts, and 5 percent raise vegetables. These farms rely heavily on a complex system of pipelines, ditches, and tributaries for freshwater irrigation.

MURRAY-DARLING WATER USE

- Livestock and crop farms used 7,720 gigaliters* of water in 2006.

- This amount is 83 percent of the total freshwater withdrawal in the basin; the rest is used by businesses (10 percent) and residents (7 percent).

- The largest agricultural water users by products include cotton (20 percent), dairy farming (17 percent), other livestock (17 percent), and rice (16 percent).

- Between 2001 and 2006, the agricultural output in the basin increased by 7.3 percent, to $15 billion a year, which is 39 percent of the total Australian agriculture industry.

*Note: 1 gigaliter = 264,172,052 U.S. gallons.

Source: Water and the Murray-Darling Basin. Australian Bureau of Statistics, 2008.

Pollution and Damage

The natural cycles of flooding in the Murray-Darling Basin have been altered by drought and as a result of regional dependence on freshwater withdrawals. Of the twenty-one rivers within the basin, all but one, the Paroo River, have been severely altered by 1,079 miles (1,736 kilometers) of human-made channels, 178 miles (286 kilometers) of levees, and 215 miles (346 kilometers) of illegal water channel diversions. This system has impacted the adjacent natural communities.

There have been documented wetland and forest losses, especially of large river red gum (*Eucalyptus camaldulensis*) stands. Known for its impressive size, the river red gum grows up to 140 feet (43 meters) tall in adjacent floodplains. High-water withdrawals and extended periods of drought have lowered water flows in the basin. As a result, the river gum trees, which are reliant on floods to germinate their seeds, cannot reproduce, and many century-old trees have died. A 2008 estimate found that 75 percent of river red gums in the Lower Murray were dying.

The Murray River town of Echuca depends on the river to attract tourists, its primary source of income. The paddle steamer industry, a main attraction for visitors, is suffering due to the extreme drought conditions affecting water levels in the area. The combination of low water levels and exposed roots has been detrimental to many large trees like this one. *(Photolibrary/Getty Images)*

In addition, wetland bird species have declined by as much as 35 percent. Up to 6,000 of the 30,000 wetlands across the basin have lost so much water that the soil chemistry has changed, resulting in shallow and stagnant pools of water and a blanket of newly created sulfuric acid-laden soils carrying a pH as low as 1.6 (7 is neutral).

The withdrawal of more than 27 percent of the basin's water each year has altered seasonal water levels. Previously, there were high flows in winter and spring and low flows in summer and fall. Irrigation for agriculture has resulted in the reverse; the low-water periods now occur in winter and spring, profoundly impacting the freshwater fisheries. Species such as the golden perch (*Macquaria ambigua*) cannot reach their traditional spawning grounds to lay and fertilize eggs in the spring due to water removals, weir placement, and larger dam construction. Additionally, a policy of removing any trees that have fallen in the rivers (often called "snags") to improve water flow has meant a substantial loss of habitat conditions essential for egg deposition and newborn fish shelter.

Bush fires across the Murray-Darling Basin are a regular component of the natural landscape. In the arid country, dry woody vegetation and trees can easily catch fire from a lightning strike. These fires result in mineral nutrients (such as nitrogran, phosphorus, and potash) being recycled into the soils, helping to reinvigorate plant growth. While this is a natural cycle, additional fires also may be caused by human carelessness. In 2003 and in 2009, there were numerous bush fires across the region.

Although a balanced ecosystem uses the water it needs and lets the remaining amount run off in adjacent waterways, a burned-over bush behaves quite differently. In 2004, muddy debris rushed off the burned sites, causing widespread erosion and a reduction in freshwater quality. By 2005, newly emergent vegetation was established and, in intense competition, thirstily consumed the limited precipitation in the area. This resulted in a 25 percent depletion of regional water flows, as seen in major droughts.

Such damage can last for a decade or more, as plants thin out and the bush takes time to restabilize. Fires that raged across Victoria in 2009 covered 1,718 square miles (4,450 square kilometers), burned down 2,050 homes, left nearly 8,100 people homeless, and took the lives of 210 people.

Mitigation and Management

Although communities hailed the River Murray Waters Agreement as an innovative approach to water management practices, decades of emphasis on dam and water control construction have severely impacted the ecology of the basin. Seventy years of altering the natural hydrology have altered the landscape of the watershed. Dried-up acid pools, abandoned salt flats, dead forests, and vacated farms are now common.

As a result, environmentalists and local residents applied pressure to local governments to enact change. The effect of this pressure began to be seen in 1984 when local governments modified the 1915 water agreement to undertake environmental efforts to restore portions of the basin. The overarching challenges were twofold: Protect the environment and provide sufficient freshwater resources for the people.

In 1985, government stakeholders coalesced their economic and environmental visions and formed the Murray-Darling Agreement to begin carrying out multiple tasks. Signed in 1987 by the federal government and the states of New South Wales, Victoria, and South Australia, this document provided a framework for redesigning the system of natural resource management and water distribution. One of the primary goals was to improve the health of both the adjacent wetlands and floodplains. At about the same time, the government also

KEY ACCOMPLISHMENTS OF THE MURRAY-DARLING BASIN COMMISSION

- Ensured delivery of water supplies in communities during the sixth year of severe drought, the worst in 113 years.

- Limited water use to 1993 levels to conserve resources.

- Signed a memorandum with the Murray-Lower Darling Rivers Indigenous Nations to work more closely on water management and environmental goals.

- Constructed new fishways at dams and other structures to boost native fish populations.

- Released water into 138 square miles (357 square kilometers) of floodplains to help encourage fish spawning, bird breeding, and vegetation restoration.

Source: Murray-Darling Basin Commission Annual Report, 2007.

launched a campaign to educate the public about the importance of balancing water withdrawals and environmental protection.

Beginning in 2000 and still ongoing in 2010, a recent period of prolonged drought has resulted in an economic and environmental crisis. Fish populations plummeted, which had an economic impact on freshwater fish markets across the country. A number of farms growing rice and wheat, staple crops in the region, failed from the lack of freshwater for irrigation.

The Murray-Darling Commission, an entity formed to carry out basin resource management goals, implemented a number of critical water management programs. The commission placed a cap on the amount of water that could be withdrawn by each community. It oversaw the installation of salt interception equipment, which pumps up groundwater, filters out the salts, and returns it to the aquifers, and thus removed half a million tons of salt from waterways.

The commission also enacted a new system of water trade among the communities of New South Wales, South Australia, and Victoria that allowed for more efficient water use and exchange, especially during an ongoing drought. And it organized a program of government "buyback" of water rights for small and large landowners. This program provides a payment, good for one year, to a farmer or business to get them to not exercise water rights or to lower their water use. In 2008, the commission was dissolved to form a single government agency, the Murray-Darling Basin Authority, to oversee the integrated planning and management of the water resources of the basin.

The most noticeable program was the restoration plan for the Murray River. The releasing of an additional 109 million gallons (413 million liters) of surface water each year, beginning in 2009, directly into wetlands and floodplains already has led to improvement in the stands of river red gums, as well as in the breeding populations of wetland species.

In 2008, rare heavy rains created a moderate flood in Queensland, followed by water pushing over riverbanks into adjacent floodplains. Instead of manipulating water levels on the Darling River, managers allowed much of the flood to occur, turning a 165-foot-wide (49-meter-wide) river into a series of floodplains up to 16 miles (26 kilometers) across. Within days, swamps near the Queensland and New South Wales border showed signs of plant regrowth.

As a result, insects that had been lying dormant in the soils came to life and multiplied in the warm conditions, providing abundant food for birds and fish. Birds such as the white-necked heron (*Ardea pacifica*) and the royal spoonbill (*Platalea regia*) established nests. (These birds, in particular, rely on the biotic boom of a flood to provide sufficient food to rear their young.) Vegetation along the floodplains sprung to life, including the first new tree seedlings in at least a decade.

Although the 2008 flood was transformative and offered encouraging short-term signs of life in the basin, the continuing drought has inflicted widespread ecological and financial damage to the area known as Australia's Mississippi. Despite ongoing conservation and resource management efforts, these impacts may take decades to overcome.

Selected Web Sites

Australian Conservation Foundation Wetlands Report: http://www.acfonline.org. au/articles/news.asp?news_id=2037&c=32333.

Australian National Water Initiative: http://www.nwc.gov.au/www/html/117-national-water-initiative.asp.

Murray-Darling Basin Authority: http://www.mdba.gov.au.

Murray-Darling Basin Documentary: http://www.abc.net.au/catalyst/murraydarling/.

Murray-Darling Basin Tour: http://www.mdbc.gov.au/about/tour_the_basin.

Save the Murray Initiative: http://www.savethemurray.com.

South Australian Museum Exhibit on Ngurunderi: http://www.samuseum.sa.gov. au/ngurunderi/ngframe.htm.

Further Reading

Australian Department of Environment and Water Resources. *National Action Plan for Salinity and Water Quality.* Sydney, Australia, 2000.

Botterill, Linda Courtenay, and Melanie Fisher. *Beyond Drought: People, Policy, and Perspectives.* Collingwood, Australia: CSIRO, 2003.

Connell, Daniel. *Water Politics in the Murray-Darling Basin.* Annandale, Australia: Federation, 2007.

Draper, Robert. *Australia's Dry Run.* Washington, DC: National Geographic, 2009.

Moles, Sarah, et al. *Wetlands For Our Future.* Carlton, Australia: Australian Conservation Foundation, 2008.

Murray-Darling Basin Commission. *Rivers as Ecological Systems: The Murray-Darling Basin.* Collingwood, Australia: CSIRO, 2001.

9 Santiago Chile

Tucked in a bowl-shaped valley in central Chile, the city of Santiago is a modern metropolis that has undergone considerable population growth and economic development since the mid-twentieth century. Chile's capital has transformed itself from a rural outpost into a modern industrial city of 7.2 million residents.

Santiago sits in the heart of the long, slender country of Chile. This nation is 2,485 miles (3,998 kilometers) long north to south, and its average width is 110 miles (177 kilometers). Spread across a 247-square-mile (640-square-kilometer) plateau at 1,706 feet (520 meters) in elevation, Santiago is bordered on the east by the Andes Mountains and on the west by the Chilean Coastal Mountains and, eventually, the Pacific Ocean. While the city is surrounded by mountains, it is dominated on its eastern boundary by the high peaks of the Andes. Two of the most prominent peaks, Mount Tupungato (21,555 feet, or 6,570 meters) and Cerro El Plomo (17,795 feet, or 5,424 meters), are clearly visible from downtown.

The region sits at the intersection of two tectonic plates. Because the Pacific Ocean's Nazca Plate is sliding under the South American Plate, the area experiences regular earthquakes. Twenty-two large-scale events, above 7.1 in magnitude on the Richter Scale, have occurred since 1570. A massive 8.8 magnitude earthquake—the seventh strongest ever recorded—occurred on February 27, 2010, approximately 200 miles (322 kilometers) southwest of Santiago. The earthquake, which lasted three minutes, killed 486 people and severely damaged 240,000 buildings.

Santiago features a mild climate (similar to the Mediterranean region) buffered by arid lands both to the north (northern Chile and central Brazil) and to the south (Antarctica). Summers, from December through March, host temperatures around 80 degrees Fahrenheit (27 degrees Celsius), and winters, from June through August, average around 57 degrees Fahrenheit (14 degrees Celsius). The region receives approximately 14 inches (36 centimeters) of rain per year, similar to western American states such as Colorado. Winters are wetter than the typically hot, dry summers. Santiago is divided in half by the Mapocho River, which is fed by glacial runoff and originates 45 miles (72 kilometers) to the east.

The city has built a state-of-the-art infrastructure for its residents, including roads, bridges, and an urban layout of buildings large and small. Central to this infrastructure is a modern freshwater delivery and management system, able to reach 100 percent of municipal households. The city has forty-four water districts that supplied up to 1.2 trillion gallons (4.5 trillion liters) of freshwater through 7,767 miles (12,497 kilometers) of pipeline in 2007. A private company, Aguas Andinas, owns and manages the citywide water and sanitation services.

One of Santiago's benefits is its proximity to the Andean Glaciers. Chile has the third-largest glacier fields in the world, after Canada and Argentina. Climate

SANTIAGO'S PUBLIC WATER SYSTEM FACTS AND FIGURES

- 86 percent of Santiago's freshwater comes from high-elevation mountain surface runoff primarily from snow- and glacier melt.

- 13 percent of the freshwater is derived from local precipitation accessed through several dozen groundwater wells.

- The city used 1.03 trillion gallons (3.9 trillion liters) of freshwater in 2003 and 1.2 trillion gallons (4.5 trillion liters) in 2007, an increase of almost 17 percent.

- Aguas Andinas, a private company, operates the water and sewer systems and serves 1.6 million residential and business connections across an area that spans 270 square miles (699 square kilometers).

Sources: Aguas Andinas and Santiago City Government, 2008.

change, however, has created a rapid rate of mountain glacial ice melting, posing a serious threat to the longevity of the freshwater supply for the city.

Human Uses

The Santiago Basin was historically inhabited by native peoples called the Mapuche (*Mapu* meaning "earth" and *Che* meaning "people"), descendants of the first people who migrated into the Americas from Siberia, approximately 11,000 years ago. To the south, archeologists excavated caves, finding evidence from up to 8,600 years ago of "hunter-picker" settlements that relied on spears to kill game such as the sloth-like milodon (*Mylodon listai*) and the American horse (*Parahipparion saldasi*), which are both now extinct.

At their greatest population before Europeans arrived, nearly 500,000 Mapuche were spread across the region, living in small, family-based groups that relied on subsistence farming, hunting, and fishing. Known as fierce warriors, several bands of Mapuche were able to defeat Inca invaders from the north circa 1450 by luring their opponents into narrow valleys, where they could attack from above.

The Spanish, led by the explorer Pedro de Valdavia, arrived in the area in 1541. Settlers established the city of Santiago on a strategic plateau. The Mapuche and Spanish fought over these lands, and de Valdavia was captured and beheaded in an insurrection in 1553. Despite the arrival of a large population of Spanish, conflict between natives and settlers continued well into the twentieth century.

In 1818, Chile gained its independence from Spain, and the young nation endured a civil war in 1891. Several governments followed, including a parliamentary democracy (1890), a Marxist state (1920s), a military dictatorship (1973–1990), and, finally, a social democracy (1991–present). After seventeen years of dictatorship, constitutional revisions now provide civilian control over the military and limited government political terms.

Until the 1940s, Santiago had little trade with other nations and relied on an agriculture-based economy. Through several free trade agreements and widespread international investments, Chile has slowly developed into a Western market economy with substantial industrial development. Part of the economic stability has come from its integration of new technologies, as well from mining mineral-rich deposits of nitrates and copper, $33 billion of which were exported in 2008.

The city of Santiago has benefited considerably from this stability. As a central city, it contains a number of high-rise buildings, as well as a modern road network and an underground commuter train system. Economic trade with the United States, Europe, and Asia has led to considerable growth in financial services,

AGUAS ANDINAS GROWS IN SANTIAGO

Indicator	2003	2007
Residents receiving freshwater	1.4 million	1.6 million
Company net annual income	$111 million	$157 million
Wastewater sewage treated	3% *	72%

This figure is for 1999; 2003 number not available.

Source: Annual Report. Aguas Andinas, 2008.

manufacturing, and retail business. Hosting the South American headquarters for several international high-tech companies also has provided an economic boost.

These circumstances have supported considerable population growth since 1940, when Santiago housed 982,000 residents. By 1970, the city had grown to 2.8 million; by 1992, it had swelled to 4.7 million. In 2009, Santiago contained approximately 7.2 million residents, representing 42 percent of Chile's total population.

Along with growth has come considerable freshwater needs. A city-wide water utility, Empresa de Agua Potable de Santiago, was established in 1861. By 1894, several reservoirs and holding tanks had been built to supply water to residents in the downtown region. In 1917, a 60-mile (97-kilometer) pipeline was laid from the mountains into the city, locally bypassing polluted waterways and ensuring a direct water supply.

The first water treatment plant, Las Vizcachas, was completed in 1969; it was followed by additional plants in 1984 and 1999. By 1993, the first sewage treatment plant was built, and new plants were built every year from 2001 to 2006.

Since 2003, the water utility Aguas Andinas has invested $285 million in modernizing freshwater delivery and sewage treatment systems. In 2007 alone, the company spent $64.2 million on construction projects: 44 percent on water systems, 46 percent on sewer systems, and 10 percent on system operations.

Pollution and Damage

The Spanish Empire established the city of Santiago as a colonial outpost almost five centuries ago based on its mild climate, productive farmlands, and plentiful freshwater supply. The city has grown steadily, particularly since the 1950s, becoming an urban metropolis and manufacturing center for much of South America.

But transforming into a large city also has brought considerable environmental challenges. Air pollution has been persistent. Some winter days, high-elevation cold air traps warm air in the valley, and the resultant thermal inversion covers Santiago in a brown cloud of smog. Regional pollution from vehicles and factories accumulates to unhealthy levels; this includes lead pollution (often from gas emissions (leaded gas was not banned until 2006) and pollution from copper smelters, which emit high levels of arsenic, sulfur dioxide, and particulates.

Another problem has to do with persistent water pollution. The city only recently has invested in sewage treatment plants, a major step toward not relying on the Mapocho River as a sewer, as it had for generations. In 2007, although 98 percent of the sewage was collected, only 72 percent of it was purified before it was released back into the Mapocho River, resulting in pollution of local waterways. Santiago also has experienced rapid population growth, and the expansion of the city's footprint has led to sprawl and suburban development, often poorly planned.

In addition, Santiago is heavily reliant on mountain runoff for its freshwater supplies. Up to 86 percent of the surface water used in Santiago originates in the mountains. A severe drought in 1969 occurred after the high-altitude snowpack over the two previous years was not up to the usual levels and provided less precipitation than expected.

The Mapocho River, running through the heart of Santiago, Chile, is contaminated by household, agricultural, and industrial sewage, as well as by upstream copper-mining waste (from the several copper mines in the Andes, east of Santiago), being dumped unfiltered into the river. Aguas Andinas, the company that provides the city's water and sanitation systems, is working on a series of an underwater pipes to collect wastewater and transport it to treatment facilities across the city. *(Bloomberg/Getty Images)*

In fact, climate change has been one of the greatest impacts on this water supply. Warming air temperatures, especially at high altitudes, have led to the loss of significant portions of the glaciers that sit atop the Andes Mountains. The Echaurren Glacier, located 21 miles (34 kilometers) east of Santiago and the source of 70 percent of the region's freshwater, has been losing up to 39 feet (12 meters) of ice per year since 1970 and is forecast to melt entirely by 2058. Juncal Sur Glacier lost an average of 164 feet (50 meters) of ice per year between 1955 and 1997. And the Grey Glacier has lost 1.8 miles (2.9 kilometers) of ice since 1985.

Up to half of the 120 glaciers in the Andes Mountains are shrinking twice as fast as they were in the late 1990s. A 2009 study by the Chilean General Water Directorate, which studied 100 of the area's 1,720 glaciers, concluded that 92 percent of the country's glaciers were shrinking, confirming that communities needed to plan for alternate long-term reliable freshwater supplies.

Mitigation and Management

In most towns and cities around the world, government agencies provide freshwater to residents and businesses. Santiago relies on a unique administration of its freshwater services and sewage management. Since the late 1980s, the entity that has provided these services to city residents has evolved from a purely government division to a hybridized public-private operation to one that is privatized and majority owned and run by an international corporation reliant on shareholders and profits.

In the late 1980s, the city's water supply system was run by Empresa Metropolitana de Obras Sanitarias, a government entity that was considered top-heavy, with too many employees, and was unable to meet the needs of a growing urban community. Concerns about corruption and poor water system mainte-ance led the government to consider privatizing the system. In a surprising resolution, in 1989 the Chilean federal government instead created a regulatory framework that was structured like a private model but was still a public entity. It created thirteen state-owned regional companies that could charge rates that reflected their actual costs instead of the previously subsidized rates.

In 1999, the Santiago freshwater utility, by far the largest in the country, was privatized. Agbar and Suez Environment, two water supply companies based in Spain, together purchased 51 percent of the utility for $2.4 billion, forming a new company named Aguas Andinas

The supporters of this controversial private ownership model conclude that the operation is much more efficient than the previous state-run system. Propo-nents highlight the number of increased investments to upgrade and provide water and sewers to areas without service. They also note the reduction in employees (from a high of 3,500 to approximately 1,400 as of 2009).

Critics of the private system blame it for up to 50 percent higher water charges passed on to citizens since 1999. They also criticize a private entity that does not have to comply with the requirements of a public one. They insist that a private company's bottom line—profit to shareholders—makes every decision accountable to only a small group of business executives and not to the public or the environment.

Despite these differing opinions, the private water and sewer business in Santiago generally is considered well run and a success. Corruption has been limited, and traded freshwater rights (shares of surface water or groundwater that can be sold) have been exposed to a healthy market, versus a monopoly. Service to homes and businesses is at an all-time high. Although costs may be higher, residents are obtaining more for their dollar than they did under a government-run system. Finally, there have been several noteworthy environmental improvements in cleaning up local waterways by reducing the release of raw sewage and capturing business pollution that used to be piped straight into adjacent rivers.

This privatization model also has been used in Chile's telecommunications, sanitation, and energy industries. Other nations have followed suit in terms of freshwater management, and 60 percent of water utilities in South American countries were privatized as of 2009. By comparison, in the United States, 15 percent of water utilities are run by private companies.

In the meantime, the emergent crisis of melting glaciers poses a very real threat to the sustainability of freshwater resources for Santiago and all of Chile. This issue has propelled government leaders to seek solutions.

In 2008, Chile's federal government adopted a national plan of action against climate change, supporting research on renewable energy technologies to reduce carbon emissions. The plan also supports the enhanced study of glaciers and proposes a number of responses to reduced drinking water availability. Possible solutions that are being evaluated include the construction of a series of new reservoirs and a network of desalination plants along the Pacific Ocean.

Selected Web Sites

Chile Air Pollution: http://www1.american.edu/TED/chileair.htm.
Glacier Shrinkage Study: http://iahs.info/hsj/506/50601.pdf.
The World Bank, Reforming the Urban Water System in Chile: http://go.worldbank.org/Q8CQNLDT50.
The World Bank, Report on the Chile Water Supply: http://rru.worldbank.org/documents/publicpolicyjournal/255Bitra-031103.pdf.

Further Reading

Aguas Andinas. *Annual Report for Santiago, Chile.* Santiago, Chile: Aguas Andinas, 2007.

Bauer, Carl. *Siren Song: Chilean Water Law as a Model for International Reform.* Washington, DC: RFF, 2004.

Bitrán, Gabriel A., and Eduardo P. Valenzuela. *Water Services in Chile.* Washington, DC: The World Bank, 2003.

Clarke, George R.G., Katrina Kosec, and Scott Wallsten. *Has Private Participation in Water and Sewerage Improved Coverage?* Washington, DC: The World Bank, 2004.

Knight, Peter G., ed. *Glacier Science and Environmental Change.* Malden, MA: Blackwell, 2006.

Seidenstat, Paul. *Reinventing Water and Wastewater Systems: Global Lessons in Improving Water Management.* New York: John Wiley and Sons, 2002.

United Nations. *Chile Water Resources.* Jeju, Republic of Korea: Final Report from the Eighth Special Session of the Global Ministerial Environment Forum: Environmental Dimension of Water, Sanitation, and Human Settlements, 2004.

FRESHWATER
CONCLUSION

10 | Water Challenges

In 2009, daily global freshwater consumption reached 9.8 trillion gallons (37 trillion liters), which was used by 6.8 billion people. Due to widespread differences in availability, wealth, and technology, much of this water was consumed by industrial nations. Technological improvements in underdeveloped countries, such as equipment to drill wells that can reach deep, remote areas and more powerful pumps, are slowly changing these disparities.

Widespread emergent threats, however, are water pollution and overextraction. Pollution from industrial and residential activity has impacted great quantities of freshwater and threatened human and biotic health. Microbial contamination, for example, has resulted in the annual deaths of up to 15 million children under five years of age. In addition, too much freshwater is being removed faster than natural recharge rates. By 2050, upwards of 2 billion people are expected to face critical water shortages.

Freshwater Wars

Population growth impacts and related freshwater problems have played a role in pushing many nations into armed conflict. In thirty-seven instances since 1950, two or more nations have gone to war over freshwater resources. Many of these disputes began over unequal water withdrawals from a shared resource. Although oil and land disputes were the source of several wars in the twentieth century, water may very well become a more common source of international conflict as the twenty-first century advances.

In 1967, the Six Day War—an armed conflict between Israel and the neighboring states of Egypt, Jordan, and Syria that lasted from June 5 through 10—was directly related to land and water issues in the Middle East. Israel increased its water withdrawals from the Jordan River in 1964 to meet its needs as a growing nation; the country distributed the water through a system of canals and pipes. Syria and Jordan also used water from the same river.

Syria and Jordan responded in 1965 to the Israeli increase in water withdrawals by beginning to build a diversion system to reduce the water available to the Israelis by at least 35 percent. This resulted in Israel bombing the diversion project in 1965 and, when the Six Day War commenced in 1967, capturing the adjacent Golan Heights from Syria in a number of days. The heights, a 690-square-mile (1,787-square-kilometer) mountainous plateau, contains a portion of the Jordan River and receives considerable water runoff from melting snow in the adjacent mountainous areas. In 2006, it was estimated that 15 per-

The historic town of Hasankeyf is one of the many civilizations at the epicenter of controversy over the building of the Ilisu Dam on the Tigris River in Turkey, a part of the Southeastern Anatolia Project. Work on the dam came to a halt in 2009 when European nations withdrew financing, citing the fact that the project was not meeting agreed-upon standards in terms of environmental and social impacts. *(Scott Peterson/Getty Images)*

WATER CONFLICTS

Countries	Water Resources	Year: Nature of Conflict
Ecuador, Peru	Cenepa River	1995: Control over headwaters/ border dispute
Kyrgyzstan, Kazakhstan	Syr Darya River	2000: Irrigation disputes and debts
Kashmir, India	Numerous streams	2002: Irrigation disputes over withdrawals
Sudan, Darfur	Wells	2003: Ethnic conflict/well poisoning
Ethiopia, Kenya	Omo River	2006: Severe drought, domestic supplies

Source: Water Conflict Chronology. Pacific Institute for Studies in Development, Environment, and Security, 2008.

cent of Israel's water supply came from this region. Although Syria continues to claim this plateau as its historic land, Israel also claims ownership of this strategic resource-rich area.

Another conflict, between Turkey, Syria, and Iraq over freshwater in the Euphrates River, has existed for hundreds of years but worsened since the early 1990s. The Euphrates originates in Turkey and travels 1,728 miles (2,780 kilometers) through Syria and Iraq before terminating in the Persian Gulf. In 1988, Turkey announced a plan for development along the river. Known as the Southeastern Anatolia Project, it committed $36 billion to building new irrigation systems, twenty-two dams, nineteen hydroelectric power-generating facilities, and other infrastructure for 9 million residents in a rural part of the southeastern country. The progress of this planned development, however, has been slowed by both internal and external conflicts.

Within Turkey, the Kurdistan Workers' Party (known as the PKK), a separatist organization that has engaged in an armed insurgent campaign since the 1970s, carried out several attacks on dams in the 1990s. With as many as 5,000 members, the party led a widespread sabotage campaign focused on areas where the Turkish government sought to boost the nation's infrastructure, such as a rural project where electricity would be generated by dams. These PKK efforts slowed construction and led to dozens of deaths and millions of dollars of property damage.

The countries of Syria and Iraq, which historically have been enemies, unified to object to Turkey's unilateral actions to limit the flow of the Euphrates River. In 1990, Turkey stopped almost the entire flow of the river in order to fill a reservoir in front of the newly built Atatürk Dam, an earth- and rock-filled dam with an embankment 604 feet (184 meters) high and 5,971 feet (1,820 meters) long that was built on the Euphrates and Tigris rivers. In response, both Syria and Iraq began to make plans to attack Turkey. After three weeks of terse exchanges and many threats, Turkey responded by once again allowing water to flow unrestricted.

In 2007, the Southeastern Anatolia Project reached the 60 percent completion mark. When the water component of the project is brought online—possibly by 2011—the flow of the Euphrates is anticipated to drop by up to 40 percent below its 1980s historic levels. This loss of water is expected to bring strong responses from both Syria and Iraq against Turkey.

As a critical resource, water use is expected to be a flashpoint for two or more nations in the years to come. The United Nations, in identifying some 300 different conflicts over the past century directly related to water removals from shared sources, predicts a rise in aggression as supplies become less available.

Water Pollution Problems

Worldwide efforts to regulate and clean up freshwater pollution emerged as a major trend in the last three decades of the twentieth century. The establishment of new laws and policies has resulted in cleaner waterways, especially in developed countries. Governments have been able to require polluters to limit toxins, better manage industrial releases, or remove toxins from waste processes.

Often, water pollution is tackled in two steps. The first challenge is to address pollution at "point" sources, such as sewer outfall pipes and factory emissions. The second challenge, which is harder to address, is to limit "non-point" pollution, such as agricultural runoff and storm water discharges.

In 2004, the United Nations estimated that up to 5.1 million adults die each year due to polluted water, sickened by chemical waste, detergents, fertilizers, heavy metals, herbicides, insecticides, oil products, sediment, and trash in the waterways. Up to 14 billion pounds (6.4 billion kilograms) of untreated human sewage and 19 trillion gallons (72 trillion liters) of liquid waste enter freshwater bodies annually.

While there has been measurable progress in capturing and treating human waste, controlling farm runoff, and limiting hazardous waste releases, the problem of water pollution continues to loom as a persistent threat to humans and the environment in both wealthy and poorer countries. Around the world, economic profit often is a higher priority than environmental protection.

The United States

Water pollution control is a recurring challenge even for the most developed countries. The U.S. government took steps to improve freshwater quality when it passed the federal Water Pollution Control Act in 1948 and the Clean Water Act in 1972. These were followed by successive reauthorizations and amendments that mandated comprehensive programs for eliminating or reducing the pollution of interstate waters and tributaries and improving the sanitary condition of surface and underground waters.

The agency charged with implementing such laws, the U.S. Environmental Protection Agency (EPA), produced the report *National Water Quality Inventory* in 2002 to assess how pollution control efforts were progressing. According to the report, up to 45 percent of rivers and streams and 47 percent of lakes still were "not clean enough to support uses such as fishing and swimming." The most common problems included atmospheric deposition (air pollution, such as sulfuric acid, that ends up in water), farm runoff, industrial pollution, and hydrologic modifications to water bodies.

Although lakes and ponds primarily were threatened by nutrients and organic enrichment such as nitrates and phosphorus, rivers and streams faced different issues such as habitat damage, sediment accumulation, and pathogen invasion, that is, accumulation of bacteria such as E. coli. Even many remote freshwater sources demonstrated the presence of pollution.

A 2006 study by the U.S. Geological Survey, a government multi-disciplinary scientific research organization, of the Lake Champlain basin in northern Vermont found an array of manufactured chemicals in the lake and adjacent rivers. The sixty-two chemicals discovered included caffeine, detergents, fire retardant, fragrances, oils, and pesticides. Although municipal sewage treatment is widely used and regulated in the basin, these and other chemical substances are not removed during the process. While most of the pollutants were found in relatively low concentrations, such as a few parts per billion, the accumulation could be considered harmful to both humans and the freshwater environment. Despite the high level of water protection efforts, these substances continue to infiltrate the natural environment. In 2008 alone, 19.5 million Americans became sick due to unclean freshwater, including contamination by bacteria, parasites, viruses, and pollution.

The long-term commitment to implement freshwater protection efforts is a challenge for the U.S. federal government and industries alike. Between 2004 and 2009, the EPA recorded 506,000 incidents of violations of the Clean Water Act by 23,000 companies. Although most of the incidents were self-reported by the polluter, government regulators pursued less than 3 percent of these violations with a monetary fine, due to lenient enforcement policies.

In 2008, the Safe Drinking Water Act—a law that outlines limits of chemical levels in public freshwater—was violated by 40 percent of the permitted systems (mostly municipal and county government freshwater providers) at least once, leading 23 million people to consume unsafe freshwater. Under federal law, states can implement the act, and forty-six states perform this function for the federal government.

Many lapses in oversight are tied to poorly managed and underfunded waste-management programs. One example, in West Virginia shows how freshwater from wells easily can become contaminated with industrial pollution. In 1997, three coal companies (Loadout, Pine Ridge, and Remington Coal) near the capital, Charleston, began disposing of their waste slurry, a by-product of washing coal, by pumping it in liquid form into nearby underground wells. This slurry is high in dissolved metals and minerals such as arsenic, barium, lead, manganese, and nickel. This practice, which was permitted by government regulators, assumed that the groundwater would dilute any toxic materials. For example, EPA records from an 8-mile (13-kilometer) area show that coal companies injected some 1.9 billion gallons (7.2 billion liters) into the ground between 2004 and 2009.

This practice resulted in severe groundwater pollution and plumes of toxins traveled miles to seep into private wells. The pollution, caused numerous skin rashes, cancer, nervous system disorders, and kidney damage; a group of 264 homeowners filed a lawsuit against the three coal companies in 2005. Up to 93 percent of the slurry, records prove, had illegal concentrations of chemical and metals, sometimes exceeding acceptable limits by 1,000 percent. The state and federal regulators admitted that they had overlooked the coal company reports while fining 4,200 violations at other mines around the state since 2000. A state-wide moratorium on permitting this type of pollution (called an injection permit) is in place, and a public water pipeline is being built to replace the contaminated well water as the community's freshwater source.

Indonesia

Some of the poorest nations in the world require international assistance to address freshwater pollution problems. Indonesia's 200-mile-long (322-kilometer-long) Citarum River runs through West Java, navigating a watershed of 5,100 square miles (13,209 square kilometers) of woodlands, farms, and cities. It eventually empties into the Java Sea. The Citarum is the largest provider of freshwater for up to 14 million area residents, supplying nearly 80 percent of the region's needs, but it also has become a pollution dumping ground, following a surge in population and industrial development.

The river often can be smelled before it is seen. It is full of floating trash and untreated human waste. Up to 2,000 factories straight-pipe their industrial waste into it, including dyes, heavy metals, paints, and other toxic brews. Farms dispose animal waste, herbicides, and pesticides into its waters. Major stretches of the river are entirely devoid of fish and other living creatures. In fact, the Citarum was recently cited as one of the most polluted rivers on Earth.

In 2008, the West Java government secured a $500 million loan from the Asian Development Bank to begin a long-term cleanup plan. Local residents have protested the large sum being borrowed because of concerns over the funds being consumed by other priorities in the corrupt government. The West Java Water Council, a panel made of up experts and community members charged with executing the plan, was formed in 2009 to help ensure an equitable distribution of funds for projects that include storm water treatment systems, sanitation projects to treat human waste, and enforcement and educational programming to halt illegal trash and toxic dumping. The fifteen-year project to clean up the locally named "river of rubbish" also is expected to relocate up to 900 residents from the river's floodplains.

Impacts From Dams

Over the course of human development, water control structures have played a central role in the advancement of societies. Communities that developed sufficient freshwater sources—by building canals, channels, or watercourses;

The Three Gorges Dam on the Yangtze River in China is the world's largest electricity-generating plant. The building of the dam was and remains controversial, as it has flooded archaeological sites, displaced over a million people, eliminated plant and animal habitats, and continues to cause ecological changes in the region. (Kim Steele/The Image Bank/Getty Images)

reservoirs, where water is collected and stored for future use; earthen dams or other barriers across watercourses to capture water; and dikes, ditches, or levees to deliver water to fields and for drinking water—prospered and grew.

One historical example is the great civilization of ancient Rome. The central aqueduct system for the city of Rome, made up of eleven large stone transport systems built over a 500-year period, between 312 B.C.E. and 226 C.E., displayed a feat of impressive engineering.

Today, there are 45,000 large dams taller than 49 feet (15 meters) high worldwide. These structures have been used to alter freshwater surface flows with a threefold purpose: to impound water for public use, to provide flood control, and to generate electricity. Internationally, these dams provide 19 percent of total global electricity. In the United States, there are 6,575 large dams that use 131 billion gallons (496 billion liters) of water each day to provide 10 percent of the nation's electricity.

Despite obvious economic and social benefits, some hydrologic structures, particularly dams, due to their ability to impound large quantities of water, have posed considerable environmental damage, both locally and regionally. One immediate impact of a dam is flooding caused by water held upriver. Up to 154,440 square miles (400,000 square kilometers) of upland (about the size of Spain) have been flooded worldwide by the creation of reservoirs upriver of dams. Where previous upland has become submerged, millions of residents have had to relocate, and many valuable plant and animal habitats have been eliminated.

Dams also reduce the flow of water downstream, which impacts the ecology and biota of the watershed. While almost all dams return water to a stream through controlled gates in the structure, the water that is released often is altered. It may

WORLD'S TALLEST DAMS

Country	Dam	Height in Feet (Meters)	Span in Feet (Meters)
China	Jinping	1,001 (305)	1,864 (568)
Tajikistan	Nurek	984 (300)	2,310 (704)
China	Xiaowan	958 (292)	2,953 (900)
Switzerland	Grand Dixence	935 (285)	2,297 (700)
China	Xiluodu	896 (273)	2,330 (710)
Georgia	Enguri	889 (271)	2,461 (750)
Italy	Vajont	856 (261)	623 (190)

Source: World Commission on Dams, 2008.

be warmer and free of sediment. Also, the release can create a current that may be stronger and cause bank erosion.

For example, before the construction of Egypt's Aswan High Dam, up to 124 million tons of river sediment flowed into the Mediterranean Sea annually. After the dam was built in 1964, 98 percent of the upriver sediment was instead held inside the Aswan Reservoir, leaving only 9.5 million tons of sediment to nourish the lower Nile River riverbeds and floodplains. This impact caused extensive downriver erosion and limited the flourishing of the Nile Delta, an ecologically rich wetland at the junction of freshwater and salt water.

The Hoover Dam, on the border between Arizona and Nevada in the United States, was built in 1935 and generates up to 2.4 megawatts of power for several western states, including Arizona, California, and Nevada. Its formation created a 247-square-mile (640-square-kilometer) body of water called Lake Mead. The lack of sediment returned to the Colorado River below the dam has caused severe erosion known as channel degradation, ranging from 10 feet (3 meters) near the dam to 1 foot (0.3 meter) 100 miles (161 kilometers) away. Although the largest in the world when it was built, the Hoover Dam now ranks thirty-fifth in size as compared to other modern dams built in the twentieth century.

The Klamath River runs 263 miles (423 kilometers) from Oregon to California. The river basin spans some 15,625 square miles (40,469 square kilometers). It starts in rich farmlands and then flows through mountains before arriving at the Pacific Ocean. The Klamath has four large dams built along its length, providing power to 70,000 homes.

Over the twentieth century, the combination of impacts from the Klamath River dams and expansive agricultural development resulted in an impaired watershed. In summer months, water temperatures often climb above 80 degrees Fahrenheit (27 degrees Celsius), causing algae blooms that, in turn, cause massive fish losses due to oxygen deprivation.

One such event in 2002 killed off some 35,000 Chinook salmon (*Oncorhynchus tshawytscha*) in the lower 40 miles (64 kilometers) of the river. In addition, the salmon have been unable to easily climb upriver to spawn, further reducing their population, which has shrunk from a high point of nearly 800,000 in the 1800s to less than one-fifth of that number in 2009. Another problem is that bacteria that thrive in the nutrient-rich waters have spread toxins that occasionally can make fish and clams dangerous to eat.

Beginning in 2002, a collaboration of farmers, members of the Yurok and Karuk tribes, fishermen, conservationists, and government regulators engaged in extensive talks to address the environmental damage. In 2005, when PacifiCorp, the owner of the dams, applied for a new fifty-year federal license, strong opposition emerged across the river basin. In 2008, the diverse collaboration formed a solution: remove certain dams and restore the river. The Klamath Basin Restoration Agreement, signed in February 2010 by the states of California and Oregon, the Klamath, Turok, and Karuk tribes, and the federal government, lays out a ten-year plan to remove four dams by 2020. Although the dam removal and habitat restoration plans are estimated to cost billions of dollars of taxpayer funds to implement, allowing the structures to stand eventually could turn the river basin into a dead zone, which would cause more economic harm.

One of the greatest impacts related to a modern dam came in 2008 when a large earthquake, measuring 8.0 in magnitude on the Richter Scale, occurred in Sichuan Province in southern China, killing some 69,227 residents and injuring 374,643 others. Several scientists concluded that the geological event was partially caused by the 320 million tons of water held back by the Zipingpu Dam, which was located 3.4 miles (5.5 kilometers) from the earthquake's epicenter. The 640 trillion pounds of weight of the water applied sufficient pressure along fault lines—nearly twenty-five times normal stresses—to hasten a quake.

The Zipingpu Dam, begun in 2001, is fifty stories, or 600 feet (183 meters), tall. Sichuan Province contains up to 400 hydroelectric dams, many of which were severely damaged by the 2008 event; Chinese officials reported that the Zipingpu Dam sustained severe, yet repairable, cracks from the quake. Since Zipingpu Dam was completed in 2004, scientists have recorded 730 local earthquakes, though most have been less than 3.0 in magnitude.

International Action Elevates Water Access

Since the late 1970s, the international community has taken significant steps to increase the availability and quality of freshwater supplies. In 1977, the United Nations hosted a water conference in Mar del Plata, Argentina; it was the first intergovernmental conference devoted exclusively to freshwater issues. A milestone in the history of water development, topics included assessments of water resources, levels of water use, and water quality. An action plan set overarching goals to increase safe drinking water and sanitation worldwide.

Three years later, the United Nations General Assembly proclaimed the 1980s to be the International Drinking Water Supply and Sanitation Decade. Urban countries planned to complete water and sanitation upgrades for 290 million residents, while rural nations set out to deliver new freshwater systems to 750 million people and new sewer systems to 300 million residents.

By 1990, a global economic recession made it clear that these goals were unobtainable, especially with limited international lending for infrastructure improvements. In 1992, the United Nations hosted the Conference on Environment and Development in Rio de Janeiro, Brazil, with a general objective "to make certain that adequate supplies of water are maintained for the entire population of the planet, while preserving the hydrological, biological, and chemical functions of ecosystems, adapting human activities with the capacity limits of nature, and combating vectors of water-related diseases." This event brought together representatives of 172 countries to discuss humans' impact on the environment and the steps needed to address unsustainable development. Water policy played a key role at these sessions.

In 1994, the International Water Resources Association, an organization formed in 1972 to promote the sustainable management of global water resources, hosted a special session at its Eighth World Water Congress held in Cairo, Egypt. This meeting resulted in a resolution to create the World Water Council, a new international group targeted at government leaders and intent on improving conservation and protection of water resources. A consensus centered around the need to create a common umbrella organization to unite the disparate, fragmented, and ineffectual efforts in global water management was established.

Headquartered in Marseilles, France, the World Water Council hosts the World Water Forum every three years. Its first major event, the 1998 International Conference on Water and Sustainable Development, was hosted in Paris, France, and was attended by representatives of eighty-four countries. Major objectives included new strategies to improve freshwater resources and better management of public water supplies, sanitation, and irrigation systems.

In 2002, the United Nations altered its legal framework concerning freshwater resources by adopting a resolution calling for freshwater to be treated as a cultural and social, rather than purely economic, good. The resolution also rejects the concept that freshwater should be traded and sold as a commodity worldwide.

That same year, the United Nations declared 2005 to 2015 an International Decade for Action called "Water for Life." In 2005, the international peacekeeping organization launched a campaign to improve delivery of clean freshwater to millions of rural areas, advance sanitation infrastructure worldwide, expand international financing to pay for projects, solve transboundary conflicts, and improve efficiency and conservation measures.

In 2006, the fourth World Water Forum was held in Mexico City. It brought together some 20,000 people from throughout the world, who participated in 206 working sessions concerning the theme "local actions for a global challenge."

In 2009, the United Nations hosted World Water Day on March 22. Culminating with a series of worldwide events, this day was given the theme "Shared Waters, Shared Opportunities" to highlight the fact that 263 bodies of freshwater cross international boundaries and that nations must work together to advance the 300 already accepted freshwater agreements among bordering countries that pledge to avoid violence and improve shared management of this critical resource.

Selected Web Sites

Atlas of International Water Agreements: http://www.transboundarywaters.orst. edu/publications/atlas/.

International Decade for Action, Water for Life (2005–2015): http://www.un.org/ waterforlifedecade/.

Pacific Institute, The World's Water: http://www.worldwater.org.

Potential Conflict to Co-operation Potential, United Nations: http://www.unesco. org/water/wwap/pccp.

Tigres-Euphrates River Dispute: http://gurukul.ucc.american.edu/ted/ice/tigris. htm.

World Water Council: http://www.worldwatercouncil.org.

Further Reading

Gleick, Peter H., et al. *The World's Water 2008–2009: The Biennial Report on Freshwater Resources.* Washington, DC: Island, 2008.

Guerquin, Francois, et al. *World Water Actions.* London, UK: Earthscan, 2003.

McCully, Patrick. *Silenced Rivers: The Ecology and Politics of Large Dams.* New York: Zed, 2001.

Priscoli, Jerome Delli. *Managing and Transforming Water Conflicts.* New York: Cambridge University Press, 2009.

Salina, Irena, ed. *Written in Water.* Washington, DC: National Geographic, 2010.

Shiva, Vandana. *Water Wars: Privatization, Pollution, and Profit.* Cambridge, MA: South End, 2002.

United Nations. *Atlas of International Freshwater Agreements.* Washington, DC: United Nations Environment Programme, 2003.

U.S. Environmental Protection Agency. *The National Water Quality Inventory.* Washington, DC: U.S. Environmental Protection Agency, 2007.

Vigil, Kenneth. *Clean Water: An Introduction to Water Quality and Pollution Control.* Corvallis: Oregon State University Press, 2003.

11 | The Water Horizon

In the late twentieth century, a loose-knit collaboration of government bureaucrats, scientists, and environmentalists raised alarms regarding human overuse of freshwater supplies and insufficient water pollution control. The worldwide population growth from 978 million people in 1800 to 6.7 billion in 2009 has resulted in a massive need for freshwater that poses considerable challenges.

Water use between 1950 and 2007 grew fourfold, to at least 3.57 quadrillion gallons (13.5 quadrillion liters) per year. With great global economic disparity, there also exists a worldwide gap in terms of daily personal water consumption (for drinking, cooking, and bathing). North Americans consume 92 gallons (348 liters) per day per person, while Europeans use 43 gallons (163 liters), and Africans in the Sahara only use 5 gallons (19 liters). Globally, agriculture consumes up to 70 percent of freshwater resources, with households using 12 percent and businesses using 18 percent.

In 2002, the World Resources Institute, a nonprofit organization dedicated to global resource and environmental policy research and analysis, developed a world map showing the water stress ratio of water use measured against available resources. The map revealed that a large portion of the planet is under high water stress. In fact, 41 percent of the world population (or about 2.9 billion people) lives in geographic areas under such water stress. There are multiple factors that influence these stress levels.

Precipitation and runoff determine surface water and groundwater supplies. Development contributes to polluted waterways. Deforestation results in in-

WORLDWIDE WATER STRESS LEVELS

Regions	Stress Level
Middle East	High
Southeast Australia	High
Central Chile	High
Western United States	High
South Africa	Moderate
Central Europe	Moderate
Central Mexico	Moderate
Southern Asia	Low
Central South America	Low
Northern Russia	Low

Source: Water Scarcity Update. World Resources Institute, 2007.

creased sediment and debris in water. The use of fertilizers, herbicides, and pesticides also has lowered the quality of waterways.

These impacts have meant that aquatic species are more imperiled than terrestrial ones. Such water-reliant species depend on moderate freshwater quality and stable environmental conditions (the water's temperature, whether it is calm or with currents, and so on); often their habitat is smaller, and it may include fewer individuals. When this limited biome is compromised with pollution or alteration, survival can become very difficult for such species.

According to the United Nations, global consumption of freshwater is expected to increase 24 percent by 2025, when the population swells to 7.8 billion people. Examples of the future "water horizon" show that many locations will need to accept supply limitations and considerably alter water use habits.

Ninety-five percent of the freshwater in the United States is held in underground aquifers. The biggest aquifer, the Ogallala (measuring 174,000 square miles, or 450,660 square kilometers), spans the central states of Nebraska and Kansas and parts of Oklahoma and northern Texas. Farms in these regions do not receive sufficient rain to grow their crops; since the late 1970s, they have been pumping freshwater from underground at a much faster rate than rain and snowmelt have replenished the shallow aquifer.

Although an estimated 33,000 trillion gallons (124,919 trillion liters) of groundwater is present in the United States, up to 3.1 trillion gallons (11.7 trillion liters) of freshwater is drawn from the Ogallala per year. Groundwater levels are dropping in the aquifer, posing a threat to the long-term sustainability of irrigation. This region contains up to 27 percent of the irrigated farmland in the country and consumes nearly 30 percent of the nation's available groundwater each year. Hydrogeologists are concerned that the rate of freshwater removal could result in pockets of poor quality, high-sodium water in the underground aquifer in some places during the next three decades.

One nation under moderate water stress is South Africa. Spanning 471,443 square miles (1.2 million square kilometers), South Africa is mostly semi-arid, fronting 1,550 miles (2,494 kilometers) of coastline from the Atlantic and Indian oceans. Average temperatures range from 50 degrees Fahrenheit (10 degrees Celsius) to 60 degrees Fahrenheit (15.6 degrees Celsius) in the winter and from 56 degrees Fahrenheit (13.3 degrees Celsius) to 69 degrees Fahrenheit (20.6 degrees Celsius) in summer. Overall, the area receives an average of only 24 inches (61 centimeters) of rain per year.

Water is scarce in the northern desert and western plateau, while the eastern and southern regions experience a more Mediterranean climate with hotter, drier summers and wetter, cooler winters. However, the overall warm conditions mean

SOUTH AFRICA'S WATER CHALLENGES

- 4 million citizens do not have access to running water in their homes; 15 million do not have adequate sanitation systems.

- Irrigation accounts for more than 62 percent of the total water use: Regional water use associations now are required to submit a water management plan to government regulators, explaining use levels, as well as conservation strategies.

- South Africa uses 74 percent of available freshwater resources annually; the adjacent countries of Botswana and Namibia use 10 percent.

- Possible sources for new water supplies include iceberg capture, desalination, and water sharing agreements with other southern countries that would allow South Africa to pump water from outside its borders.

Source: Department of Water Affairs and Forestry, Government of South Africa, 2008.

that almost all of the rainwater either evaporates into the atmosphere or is lost through runoff through rivers: Only 8 percent of precipitation collects in ponds and lakes.

South Africa experienced considerable population growth in the last two decades of the twentieth century and first decade of the twenty-first. In 1980, it contained some 28.4 million residents. By 2009, the population had grown to 47.9 million. A number of dams built for power generation have resulted in a 50 percent loss of adjacent wetland areas.

In response to these conditions, the federal government passed a Water Services Act in 1997 and National Water Act in 1998. These laws, among other regulatory measures, declared access to freshwater a human right and not a privilege. As there is more water in the eastern and southern parts of the country, the biggest issue will be to ensure that the available water supply is distributed on an equitable scale geographically. South Africa's water supply challenges are daunting, because continued population growth and economic development could translate into a 52 percent increase in freshwater needs by the year 2040.

Water Conservation

The American inventor and statesman Benjamin Franklin wrote in his 1758 essay titled "The Way to Wealth," "When the well is dry, we shall know the value of water." In 2009, nearly one-third of global nations lacked sufficient year-round water supplies, and that number is expected to grow by nearly one-half by 2025.

The water crisis stretches far and wide. In 2009, fires raged in parched southeast Australia, where a decade-long drought and over-removal of surface flows have left a barren landscape. Many other surface water supplies are shrinking. Africa's Lake Chad is one-twentieth its historic size. North America's Lake Superior, the largest body of freshwater on the planet by surface area, is experiencing its lowest water levels since 1926.

In other cases, the land itself is being altered. It was estimated in 2009 that Mexico City is sinking by an estimated 1.5 inches (38 millimeters) per year due to groundwater extractions. The land under the city of Ravenna, Italy, has been sinking since the end of World War II, by up to 0.3 inches (8 millimeters) a year, due to the removal of groundwater and natural gas.

Other freshwater sources simply have been over-tapped. Occasionally, the Colorado River is barely a stream when it reaches the Pacific Ocean, as is China's Yellow River by the time it drains to the Bohai Sea. North America's Great Lakes are shrinking in size due to water diversions and removals. In 2008, Central Asia's Aral Sea was less than one-third of its size in 1973. Retreating water levels have left some fishing vessels high and dry in a sandy desert-like landscape.

These stark images of the overuse of freshwater resources also can be found throughout local residential, industrial, or agricultural settings—up to 35 percent of water is wasted, either knowingly, particularly if water is plentiful, or unknowingly, if losses are hidden by older equipment or underground pipes. With limits to freshwater availability reported in all corners of the planet, efforts to reduce water waste and improve conservation measures have become more common since the late twentieth century.

Many government agencies and communities have responded to the issue of limited water supplies by imposing new water utility management efforts and water use restrictions. As water conservation as a practice has been described as "in its infancy," these changes can be complex and difficult to implement.

The semi-arid city of Los Angeles, located in southern California, had 4 million residents in 2009. The city receives 15 inches (38 centimeters) of rain per year and has limited surface water and groundwater supplies. Los Angeles used approximately 199 billion gallons (753 billion liters) of water in 2008, 86 percent of which came from watersheds in the distant mountains of California (the Sierras) and Colorado (the Colorado Rockies). Because it is highly reliant on outside water supplies, the city has had to limit water consumption even while recording its ongoing population growth.

Since the 1970s, water usage in Los Angeles has been kept nearly level, even though 1 million new residents have arrived during that time period. Water conservation has been accomplished through a variety of strict measures, such as limited lawn watering, programs that provide incentives for fixture (toilets, showers, and sinks) replacements, and even a ban on serving water to restaurant customers unless requested. Between 1990 and 2006, these conservation programs saved a collective 670 billion gallons of water. New conservation efforts between 2008 and 2009 resulted in a 17 percent decline of water use, mainly due to government and industry restrictions.

In the United States, only a handful of cities, mostly in the western region, are comparable to Los Angeles in its water conservation measures. For example, up to 50 percent of the 200 million toilets in the United States require in excess of 2.5 gallons (9.5 liters) for each flush; new water conservation toilets use less than 1 gallon (3.8 liters). Although such new technology is available, most households will not replace their toilets until they crack and leak, which may be decades away. Nevertheless, an increasing number of communities have responded to water scarcity by imposing steeper fees for public water usage, limiting watering of lawns and gardens, and requiring more efficient faucets, showerheads, and toilets for new construction or renovation.

In 2002, the city council of Santa Fe, New Mexico, went so far as to halt new building permits during a severe drought. The only way residential housing and commercial developers could again receive permits was to agree to offset the water used in new construction by installing water-conserving equipment and fixtures in existing homes. Residential and business water customers also were required to adhere to strict water use regulations, which effectively reduced water use by 40 percent between 1995 and 2007. Per person, water use dropped from 168 gallons (636 liters) per day in 1994 to 101 gallons (382 liters) in 2007.

Food production and processing also are considerable draws on the global freshwater supply. Irrigation systems for farms, which use 70 percent or more of global freshwater supplies, often result in considerable waste. Trenches used to transport water rarely are lined, and up to 15 percent of the water being transported is absorbed into the soil or evaporates before it reaches crops or livestock. Large sprinkler systems also can apply excessive amounts of water. In addition, once a produce item is picked, it needs to be prepared for delivery to the marketplace. Most items are washed once in the field and then a second time with industrial equipment in a processing plant that uses large amounts of water.

WATER CONSERVATION MEASURES

- In the bathroom: If your toilet uses more than 1.6 gallons (6 liters) per flush, put a plastic bottle filled with half sand and half water in the tank. This saves up to 500 gallons (1,893 liters) per year.

- In the kitchen: When washing dishes, use one sink for soapy water and a second (or small dish tub) for rinsing. This saves up to 600 gallons (2,271 liters) per year.

- In the yard: Water the lawn only when it is necessary and only twice a week with a good soaking. For a 2,500 square-foot (232-square-meter) lawn, this saves upwards of 1,000 gallons (3,785 liters) per summer.

- In addition: Install low-flow shower and faucet heads, look for rebates for other water-saving equipment that features the "Energy Star" label, such as dishwashers and washing machines, and redirect summer rainwater from gutters into a water storage barrel or tank for garden use.

In response to concerns over a lack of freshwater conservation, farms have begun to improve their water management practices, including utilizing irrigation systems that reduce overall use, applying water so that the soil absorption rate is higher, relying on rain meters to gauge when watering is needed, and limiting unnecessary site runoff. In 2002, the Mexican government invested $40 million in conservation efforts in the country's northern farms. Although farmers were at first skeptical about these efforts, voicing concern that conservation equated with removal of their water rights, they cautiously supported the project. Completed efforts included lining water trenches to make them impervious, replacing water distribution piping, and installing more efficient and directed sprinkler heads. Water use declined by nearly 15 percent per year for the two years after this conservation effort was implemented, resulting in an immediate water and monetary savings to farmers.

Another problem in food production is that up to 40 percent of what is grown spoils before it can be consumed, wasting considerable water resources. This spoilage occurs in the picking, processing, transportation, and selling stages. The common reason for this loss is the large distance that produce must travel from the field to a store. And water usage for raising livestock is far greater than that for growing vegetables. In order to grow 2.5 pounds (1.1 kilograms) of potatoes, 26 gallons (98 liters) of water is needed, whereas raising the same amount of beef requires 2,859 gallons (10,822 liters).

Additionally, restaurants are key locations for conservation measures, as they require considerable water. A 125-seat restaurant that serves 225 meals per day requires up to 200,000 gallons (757,082 liters) of water per year, or 2.4 gallons (9 liters) for each meal. In 2009, the department of public health of the city of San Francisco, California, produced a "Green Restaurant Guide" to encourage businesses to focus on Earth-friendly practices, such as water conservation.

Technology Increases Water Resources

There are 263 river basins around the world that cover 46 percent of the upland and support 40 percent of the global population. One-quarter of these basins lack sufficient current or long-term freshwater input and resources. Improvements to water-sharing agreements between bordering nations have helped distribute limited water supplies.

Emergent tools to discover and inventory water supplies have included cutting-edge technology, including computer-enhanced satellite images, thermal analysis, sonar scans, and chemical monitoring. Using these methods, scientists are better able to locate water supplies and even find hidden sources underneath layers of bedrock.

Long Island Soundkeeper Terry Backer discusses the Smart Sponge at the Maritime Aquarium in Norwalk, Connecticut. The Smart Sponge, developed by AbTech, is a cost-effective filtration system that removes harmful petroleum substances, such as debris, gasoline, grease, oil, and sediment, from freshwater or salt water and kills bacteria such as E. coli and enterococcus on contact. This system could be helpful in cleaning upland toxic waste sites or oil spills in ocean water. *(Stringer/Getty Images)*

Between 1999 and 2007, the European Space Agency has overseen a project that has studied the water resources of Nigeria in West Africa using satellite images and infrared and other scans to determine new locations for groundwater access. This approach is especially helpful during dry periods, when groundwater wells are used to supplement surface supplies.

Scientists in northern China also employed similar spaced-based satellite remote sensing technology in 2005 along the Yangtze River delta to better understand the surface water and groundwater movements, presence of silt and other sediment, and deepwater channels in the region. This information has been useful in economic development of a region that has upwards of 80 million people, many of which rely on ship access up the river for commerce.

The United Nations maintains several programs that work toward solving freshwater supply and distribution problems around the world. In 2005, the United Nations funded eighty-four hydrology research projects in fifty countries, including Bangladesh, Ethiopia, and Senegal. A portion of these projects relied on improving freshwater supplies by studying groundwater movements. Using isotope hydrology, a field team sampled surface water or groundwater supplies and analyzed the chemical content and naturally occurring radioactive isotopes (from dissolved rock). By using a combination of water science and radioactive material tracking, scientists have learned how to trace water samples to a larger source, to better understand movement patterns, and to increase freshwater availability.

All underground freshwater contains radioactive isotopes—commonly oxygen 18 and 16—that get picked up as water sits underground in rock beds. Molecular study of samples can reveal the water body's age, origins, flow rates, and even its current size. If a village has a well, researchers can tell if it contains "old" or "new" water and how much water can be pumped without running out or degrading the quality.

Given that the oceans contain 96.5 percent of the water on planet, transforming salt water into freshwater with desalination technology is an obvious solution to low freshwater supplies. Desalination uses energy to remove the salt through a process of either rapid evaporation or pressurized filtration. The process takes salt water with a sodium content of approximately 45,000 milligrams per liter and creates drinking water with levels at or below 25 to 50 milligrams per liter.

The technology, however, often requires considerable energy, such as natural gas or oil to run treatment plants, and large amounts of electricity, resulting in high monetary costs. In addition to the air pollution created by such electricity generation, traditional desalination also creates a potent briny by-product.

In 2008, there were 13,080 desalination plants located around the world in 120 countries producing 12 billion gallons (45 billion liters) of freshwater per day. Almost three-quarters of the worldwide desalination occurs in the energy-rich Middle East. The largest desalination plant, Jebel Ali located in the United Arab Emirates, produces more than 79 billion gallons (299 billion liters) of freshwater per year. By contrast, a plant built in Tampa Bay, Florida, produces 25 million gallons (95 million liters) per day, following five years of startup problems.

Looking forward, new technological improvements are expected to reduce the overall cost of desalination by 50 percent by capturing excess energy if heat is re-used in the evaporative process and using state-of-the-art filters in a process called reverse osmosis, which relies on high-pressure pumps and membrane filters to remove salts from water. Desalination plants also are working to build renewable energy–generating facilities on-site with industrial-sized wind turbines and solar panel farms, as well as to make their effluent less toxic by diluting the by-product to reduce local coastal ecological impacts.

Peak Water and the Future

During the late twentieth century, the world began to recognize that natural areas could not sustain unrestrained human impacts. Air pollution sources, both fixed and mobile, have been modified to reduce emissions. Land management and

At her office in Singapore, Olivia Lum, founder and chief executive of the water treatment firm Hyflux, operates an appliance that can extract moisture from the air and turn it into drinking water. Hyflux and its subsidiaries are leaders in the water and renewable resource management industry. *(Roslan Rahman/AFP/Getty Images)*

conservation programs have limited development and protected both upland and wetland habitat and wildlife populations. Efforts have been extended to set aside and better manage both temperate and tropical forests.

Freshwater pollution control laws and regulations, which emerged in the 1950s, have proven effective if paired with adequate governmental funding and regulation. But growing populations worldwide continue to test not only the limits of the freshwater supply but also the ability of the regulatory community to prevent pollution.

Freshwater, like many natural resources, exists in a limited supply. Scientists and economists have used the term "peak oil" to describe when a limit to the supply of petroleum resources is discovered. With broad political, economic, and social ramifications, the United States's peak oil supply reached this point in the 1970s, as oil output began to decline. The North Sea reached a peak in oil withdrawals in 2000. Peak oil is expected to be reached globally around 2020.

Knowing that a finite supply of oil exists, many governments and corporations, including oil companies, are beginning to alter their businesses, seeking new sources of energy (such as natural gas and geothermal) and investing heavily in renewable technologies (such as wind and solar). The market for oil also is particularly susceptible to impacts such as limited supplies and price spikes; the year 2008 saw the market price for oil crest at $140 per barrel, making a peak oil environment very real.

Similarly, with one-third of the world, or eighty countries, living with moderate to high stress levels for freshwater, the Pacific Institute, a California-based nonpartisan research institute, concluded in 2009 that the world is reaching a "peak water" scenario. In many regions, more freshwater is pumped from underground than is replenished. By 2025, the United Nations expects freshwater demands to have grown by 24 percent, leaving some 1.8 billion people living in conditions of "absolute water scarcity."

In 2008, global freshwater consumption was estimated at 3.57 quadrillion gallons (13.5 quadrillion liters) per year. Worldwide renewable sources of freshwater and salt water total over 328 million cubic miles (1.37 billion cubic kilometers).

The threat is not that the whole planet will "run out" of water but that freshwater supplies, especially near large population centers, will be greatly diminished, causing severe economic and social stresses. Water pollution and excessive freshwater removal poses ecological threats to animals and plants. Often by the time impacts are realized, biological and ecological losses already have occurred.

Selected Web Sites

Pacific Institute, Peak Water 2008 Keynote Address by Meena Palaniappan: http://www.pacinst.org/publications/presentation/peak_water_talk.pdf.

U.S. Government Report on Water Supply Issues: http://www.gao.gov/htext/d03514.html.

Water—Use It Wisely: http://www.wateruseitwisely.com.

Watersheds of the World: http://www.earthtrends.wri.org/pdf_library/maps/watersheds/gm16.pdf.

White Paper on Water Policy, South Africa: http://www.africanwater.org/wp3.htm.

Further Reading

Barlow, Maude. *Blue Covenant: The Global Water Crisis and the Coming Battle for the Right to Water.* New York: New Press, 2009.

Gray, N.F. *Water Technology: An Introduction for Environmental Students.* London, UK: Butterworth Heinemann, 2005.

Hammer, Mark. *Water and Wastewater Technology.* Upper Saddle River, NJ: Prentice Hall, 2007.

Lauer, William C., ed. *Desalination of Seawater and Brackish Water.* Denver: American Waterworks Association, 2006.

Lohan, Tara. *Water Consciousness.* San Francisco: AlterNet, 2008.

Palaniappan, Meena. *Peak Water.* Oakland, CA: Pacific Institute, 2008.

Pearce, Fred. *When the Rivers Run Dry: Water—The Defining Crisis of the Twenty-First Century.* Boston: Beacon, 2006.

United Nations. *Fresh Water Under Threat, Vulnerability Assessment of Freshwater Resources to Environmental Change in Africa.* Washington, DC: United Nations Environment Programme, 2009.

———. *Water: A Shared Responsibility.* Washington, DC: United Nations Environment Programme, 2006.

Acid rain. Rain or other precipitation that is unusually acidic. It is the result of emissions of carbon, nitrogen, and sulfur (typically from industry), which react with water to form acids. Acid rain causes harm to animals, plants, soils, and structures.

Algae. A diverse group of photosynthetic, single-cell, and multicellular aquatic organisms. Most algae live at or near the surface of wetlands, freshwater bodies, or oceans, and are consumed by species such as copepods. There are approximately 15,000 different species of algae worldwide.

Aquifer. An underground layer of permeable gravel, rock, soil, or sand from which groundwater can be extracted.

Arid. An excessively dry region where total precipitation is insufficient to support significant biological life or agricultural crops and livestock.

Artesian well. A well in which water rises naturally to the surface.

Atmosphere. The mixture of gases surrounding the Earth. By volume, it consists of about 78.08 percent nitrogen, 20.95 percent oxygen, 0.93 percent argon, 0.036 percent carbon dioxide, and trace amounts of other gases, including helium, hydrogen, methane, and ozone.

Bacteria. Simple, single-celled microorganisms that live in organic matter, soil, water, and the bodies of plants and animals. Some bacteria are pathogenic— that is, responsible for causing infectious diseases.

Biodiversity. Biological diversity, indicated by the variety of living organisms and ecosystems in which they live.

Biome. A regional ecosystem that is characterized by a particular climate and biological community.

Biosolids. Nutrient-rich by-products of sewage sludge, or the residue created by sewage treatment.

Biosphere. The ecological system made up of all living organisms on Earth.

Biota. The plants and animals that live in a particular location or region.

Brackish. A mixture of freshwater and salt water.

Carbon dioxide (CO_2). A gas that is found naturally in the atmosphere at a concentration of 0.036 percent. It is fundamental to life and is required for respiration and photosynthesis.

Carbon neutral. A state in which no carbon is released into the environment, achieved through a process of controlling the emission and absorption of carbon.

Carcinogen. A substance that causes cancerous growth in living tissue.

Climate change. Global variation in the Earth's climate over time. A recent phenomenon (measured over the last two centuries), it is attributable largely to human atmospheric pollution. Climate change results in temperature increases and other shifts in weather patterns, severe droughts and floods, rising sea levels, and biotic changes (often causing the loss of species in an area).

Coliform bacteria. A group of microorganisms that cause cholera and other diseases. The concentration of coliform bacteria often is used to measure the sanitary quality of a body of water.

Combined sewer overflow. A major source of water pollution that occurs when excessive flooding causes the combined wastewater of a jurisdiction, including storm water runoff, domestic sewage, and industrial wastewater, to be discharged untreated into natural waterways.

Condensation. The conversion of vapor (a gas) into a liquid or solid state; the opposite of evaporation.

Conservation. The protection, preservation, management, or restoration of natural resources, plants, and wildlife.

Contaminant. A chemical, biological, or physical substance that alters air, land, or water conditions in a negative manner.

Cryptosporidium. A microbe found in bodies of water that causes gastro-intestinal illnesses and is highly resistant to disinfectants.

Dam. A structure made of earth, rock, or concrete that is used to retain water in a lake or river.

Decomposition. The process by which organic matter is broken down by dynamic forces such as microbes, water, and weather.

Depletion. The loss of water from either surface or groundwater sources that is faster than the rate of recharge.

Dilution method. The dumping of waste into water bodies or groundwater wells, where it is diluted by the movement of water and, theoretically, made less potent.

Discharge. The release of untreated waste into waterways, often following excessive precipitation that exceeds the capacity of a sewer system or waste processing facility.

Ecosystem. The interaction of a biological community and its environment.

Effluent. The outflow of water from a wastewater treatment plant or septic tank.

Endangered (and threatened) species. A species that is in danger of extinction because the total population is insufficient to reproduce enough offspring to ensure its survival. A threatened species exhibits declining or dangerously low population but still has enough members to maintain or increase its numbers.

Endemic. A plant or animal that is native to and occupies a limited geographic area.

Environment. External conditions that affect an organism or a biological community.

Environmental Impact Statement (EIS). A report on the environmental impact of large development projects that is mandated by the U.S. government.

Environmental Protection Agency (EPA). Founded in 1970, this independent U.S. federal agency is responsible for research, education, and assessment of the nation's environment; it also develops and enforces environmental laws and regulations.

Erosion. The removal of materials from a location as a result of wind or water currents.

Eutrophication. Algae blooms in aquatic ecosystems that are caused by excessive concentrations of organic and inorganic nutrients, including garden and lawn fertilizers and sewage system discharges. These blooms reduce dissolved oxygen in the water when dead plant material decomposes, causing other organisms, such as crabs and fish, to die.

Evaporation. The process by which a liquid is converted into a vapor (gaseous) state.

Evapotranspiration. The loss of water from the soil as a result of plant transpiration and evaporation.

Flood. The sudden inundation of land with water from weather or adjacent water bodies.

Floodplains. Low-lying, flood-prone land areas that are adjacent to rivers and other waterways.

Freshwater. Water that contains less than 1,000 milligrams per liter of dissolved solids, such as metals, nutrients, salts, and other materials.

Greenhouse effect. A warming of the Earth caused by the presence of heat-trapping gases in the atmosphere—primarily carbon dioxide, methane, nitrous oxide, ozone, and water vapor—mimicking the effect of a greenhouse.

Groundwater. Water below the Earth's surface.

Groundwater recharge. The refill of an underground aquifer, often by precipitation or inflow from springs or another aquifer.

Habitat. An area in which a particular plant or animal can live, grow, and reproduce naturally.

Hazardous waste. Industrial and household chemicals and other wastes that are highly toxic to humans and the environment.

Heavy metals. Metallic elements of high density that are toxic at low concentrations (for instance, lead and mercury).

Herbicides. Chemicals that are used to kill or inhibit the growth of plants. Selective herbicides kill a specific type of plant, while nonselective herbicides kill all plants.

Hydrologic cycle. The continuous movement of water as a result of evaporation, precipitation, and groundwater or surface water flows.

Hydrology. The science of the movement and properties of water both aboveground and underground.

Infiltration. The gravity-directed movement of water through pores of rock or between soil particles.

Inorganic chemicals. Mineral-based compounds that do not contain carbon among their principal elements (such as acids, metals, minerals, and salts).

Insecticides. Chemicals used to kill insects that are harmful to agriculture or humans.

Lake. An inland body of standing water, commonly fresh, that is larger than a pond.

Liquid. One of three states (together with gas and solid) of molecular matter. Water is a solid at temperatures up to 32 degrees Fahrenheit (0 degrees Celsius), a liquid up to 212 degrees Fahrenheit (100 degrees Celsius), and a gas at higher temperatures.

Nitrates. A form of naturally occurring nitrogen that is found in fertilizers, human waste, and landfills and can cause eutrophication in wetlands and open water.

Non-point source. A source of pollution that comes from a broad area (such as car and truck emissions) rather than a single point of origin (known as a point source).

Nonrenewable resource. A natural resource that cannot be produced or regenerated at a rate high enough to sustain its consumption (such as fossil fuels).

Nutrients. Chemicals that are necessary for organic growth and reproduction. For example, the primary plant nutrients are nitrogen, phosphorus, and potassium.

Organic chemicals. A large family of carbon-based chemicals, such as methane and vitamin B. In comparison, inorganic chemicals often are mineral-based, such as chloride and sodium.

Organism. A living thing, such as a plant, fungus, microorganism, or animal.

Percolation. The downward movement of water through the subsurface of the Earth to an area of collection.

pH. A measurement of the acidity or alkalinity of a solution, referring to the potential (p) of the hydrogen (H) ion concentration. The pH scale ranges from 0 to 14; acidic substances have lower pH values, while alkaline or basic substances have higher values.

Phosphorus. An element in the nitrogen family that, in high concentrations, can cause eutrophication in a body of water.

Photosynthesis. The chemical process by which carbon dioxide and water are converted into organic compounds, primarily sugars, when the chlorophyll-containing tissues of plants are exposed to sunlight. Oxygen is released as a by-product. Photosynthesis occurs in algae, phytoplankton, plants, and some bacteria.

Point source. A source of pollution that originates from a single point, such as the discharge end of a pipe or a power plant.

Pond. A small body of standing freshwater, usually smaller than a lake.

Precipitation. Water that falls from the atmosphere in a gaseous (fog), liquid (rain), or solid (hail, ice, and snow) state.

Recharge. The process by which water is added to an aquifer.

Renewable resource. A natural resource (such as air, trees, and water) that cannot be exhausted, because it is continuously being produced.

Reservoir. A natural or manufactured body of water that stores or regulates water.

River. A moderate to large stream of water flowing from one location to another.

Runoff. Precipitation that flows overland to surface water bodies, including oceans, ponds, rivers, streams, and wetlands.

Salt water. Freshwater that contains a percentage (0.5 parts per thousand) of dissolved salt minerals.

Sanitary engineering. A scientific field specializing in environmental maintenance, usually involving the disposal of domestic and industrial waste.

Sediment. Small fragments of organic or inorganic material derived from weathered rock.

Septic tank. A tank made of concrete or fiberglass that is used to hold sewage solids, usually from individual homes. The tank and its associated pipeline distribute the liquid effluent from the tank into a leaching field, making up a septic system.

Spring. The appearance of groundwater at the surface of the land. A spring may flow with notable intensity, or it may be only a trickle.

Storm water runoff. The potent mix of dirt, nutrients, oils, and trash that is flushed from the land by rain, ending up in groundwater, lakes, oceans, ponds, rivers, streams, and wetlands.

Stream. A small to medium-sized body of water flowing through defined channels.

Taxa. The classification of organisms in an ordered, hierarchical system that indicates their natural relationships. The taxa system consists of the following categories: kingdom, phylum, class, order, family, genus, and species.

Thermal pollution. The discharge of heated or cooled water into a lake, river, stream, or other body of water, resulting in a change in ambient water temperature that is harmful to plants and animals. Such pollution is caused by the disposal of industrial wastewater or water from the cooling towers of nuclear power plants.

Total maximum daily load (TMDL). The quantity of chemicals (such as nitrogen and phosphorus) that can be discharged into a waterway from all recognized sources (such as businesses, farms, septic systems, and street runoff), while still maintaining applicable water quality standards.

Transpiration. The loss of water in the form of vapor from plant surfaces, especially the leaves, stems, and roots. The rate of transpiration is increased by temperature, wind speed, and light intensity or decreased by humidity in the surrounding air.

Turbidity. Cloudiness observed in water caused by suspended solids.

Vapor. The gaseous state of a substance.

Virus. Microorganisms (approximately 10 to 100 times smaller than bacteria) that cause infectious diseases, such as influenza and smallpox. Viruses are parasites in that they cannot replicate outside the cells of the host organism.

Water (H_2O). A tasteless, odorless liquid formed by two parts of hydrogen and one part of oxygen.

Water conservation. The careful use and protection of water resources for long-term use.

Watershed. A portion of land where all of the water runoff drains into the same body of water; also called a drainage basin.

Wetland. A low-lying area where a high level of saturation by water provides a habitat that is critical to plant and animal life.

Selected Web Sites

For additional Web Sites on more specific topics, please see the Web Site listings in individual chapters.

American Water Works Association: http://www.awwa.org.

Atlas of International Water Agreements: http://www.transboundarywaters.orst.edu/publications/atlas/.

Australian Conservation Foundation: http://www.acfonline.org.au.

Australian Government, National Water Commission: http://www.nwc.gov.au.

Baikal Watch: http://www.earthisland.org/baikal/.

European Union Water Site: http://ec.europa.eu/environment/water/index_en.htm.

Lake Baikal, United Nations World Heritage Site: http://whc.unesco.org/en/list/754.

Murray-Darling Basin Authority: http://www.mdba.gov.au.

New York City Department of Environmental Protection: http://nyc.gov/html/dep.

Pacific Institute, The World's Water: http://www.worldwater.org.

Salton Sea Authority: http://www.saltonsea.ca.gov.

U.S. Bureau of Reclamation: http://www.usbr.gov/.

U.S. Geological Survey, Water Science for Schools: http://ga.water.usgs.gov/edu.

United Nations, International Decade for Action, Water for Life (2005–2015): http://www.un.org/waterforlifedecade/.

United Nations World Water Assessment Program: http://www.unesco.org/water/wwap/.

Water—Use It Wisely: http://www.wateruseitwisely.com.

The World Bank, Nigeria Projects: http://go.worldbank.org/4ANKR2VKI0.

World Health Organization, Water, Sanitation, and Hygiene: http://www.who.int/water_sanitation_health/en/.

World Water Council: http://www.worldwatercouncil.org.

Further Reading

Aguas Andinas. *Annual Report for Santiago, Chile*. Santiago, Chile: Aguas Andinas, 2007.

Allan, Tony. *The Middle East Water Question*. New York: I.B. Tauris, 2002.

Australian Department of Environment and Water Resources. *National Action Plan for Salinity and Water Quality*. Sydney, Australia, 2000.

Barlow, Maude. *Blue Covenant: The Global Water Crisis and the Coming Battle for the Right to Water*. New York: New Press, 2009.

Bauer, Carl. *Siren Song: Chilean Water Law as a Model for International Reform*. Washington, DC: RFF, 2004.

Benjamin, Mark. *Water Chemistry*. New York: McGraw-Hill, 2001.

Bitrán, Gabriel A., and Eduardo P. Valenzuela. *Water Services in Chile*. Washington, DC: The World Bank, 2003.

Bone, Kevin, ed. *Water-Works: The Architecture and Engineering of the New York City Water Supply System*. New York: Monacelli, 2006.

Botterill, Linda Courtenay, and Melanie Fisher. *Beyond Drought: People, Policy, and Perspectives*. Collingwood, Australia: CSIRO, 2003.

Boyd, Claude E. *Water Quality: An Introduction*. Norwell, MA: Kluwer Academic, 2000.

Brutsaert, Wilfried. *Hydrology: An Introduction*. New York: Cambridge University Press, 2005.

Casey, Michael S. *The History of Kuwait*. Portsmouth, NH: Greenwood, 2007.

Cech, Thomas V. *Principles of Water Resources: History, Development, Management and Policy*. Hoboken, NJ: John Wiley and Sons, 2009.

Clarke, George R.G., Katrina Kosec, and Scott Wallsten. *Has Private Participation in Water and Sewerage Improved Coverage?* Washington, DC: The World Bank, 2004.

Connell, Daniel. *Water Politics in the Murray-Darling Basin*. Annandale, Australia: Federation, 2007.

Day, Trevor. *Water*. New York: DK, 2007.

Draper, Robert. *Australia's Dry Run*. Washington, DC: National Geographic, 2009.

Fadlelmawla, Amr, et al. *Analysis of the Water Resources Status in Kuwait*. Dordrecht, The Netherlands: Springer, Water Resources Management, 2005.

Falola, Toyin, and Matthew Heaton. *A History of Nigeria*. Cambridge, UK: Cambridge University Press, 2008.

Galusha, Diana. *Liquid Assets*. Fleischmanns, New York: Purple Mountain, 2002.

Gleick, Peter H., et al. *The World's Water 2008–2009: The Biennial Report on Freshwater Resources*. Washington, DC: Island, 2008.

Glennon, Robert. *Water Follies*. Washington, DC: Island, 2002.

Golitzen, Katherin George, ed. *The Niger River Basin: A Vision for Sustainable Management.* Washington, DC: The World Bank, 2005.

Goudie, Andrew. *The Human Impact on the Natural Environment.* Malden, MA: Blackwell, 2000.

Gray, N.F. *Water Technology: An Introduction for Environmental Students.* London, UK: Butterworth Heinemann, 2005.

Greenberg, Stanley. *Waterworks.* New York: Princeton Architectural Press, 2003.

Guerquin, Francois, et al. *World Water Actions.* London, UK: Earthscan, 2003.

Hall, Edward Hagaman. *The Catskill Aqueduct and Earlier Water Supplies of the City of New York.* 1917. Ann Arbor: University of Michigan, 2006.

Hammer, Mark. *Water and Wastewater Technology.* Upper Saddle River, NJ: Prentice Hall, 2007.

Hurlbert, Stuart, ed. *The Salton Sea Centennial Symposium.* Dordrecht, The Netherlands: Springer, 2008.

Jenkins, Mark. *To Timbuktu: A Journey Down the Niger.* New York: Modern Times, 2008.

Kennan, George. *The Salton Sea: An Account of Harriman's Fight with the Colorado River (1917).* Whitefish, MT: Kessinger, 2008.

Knight, Peter G., ed. *Glacier Science and Environmental Change.* Malden, MA: Blackwell, 2006.

Koeppel, Gerard T. *Water for Gotham: A History.* Princeton, NJ: Princeton University Press, 2000.

Kumagai, Michio, and Warwick F. Vincent, eds. *Freshwater Management.* New York: Springer-Verlag, 2005.

Kuwait Institute for Scientific Research. *Food Security and Strategic Water Reserves in Kuwait.* Safat, Kuwait: Kuwait Institute for Scientific Research, 2008.

Lauer, William C., ed. *Desalination of Seawater and Brackish Water.* Denver: American Waterworks Association, 2006.

Lohan, Tara. *Water Consciousness.* San Francisco: AlterNet, 2008.

Marks, William E., ed. *Water Voices from Around the World.* Edgartown, MA: Water Voice, 2007.

Matthiessen, Peter. *Baikal: Sacred Sea of Siberia.* New York: Random House, 1992.

McCarthy, Brendan. *Restoring the Salton Sea.* Sacramento: California Legislative Analyst's Office, 2008.

McCully, Betsy. *City at the Water's Edge.* Piscataway, NJ: Rutgers University Press, 2007.

McCully, Patrick. *Silenced Rivers: The Ecology and Politics of Large Dams.* New York: Zed, 2001.

Minoura, Koji, ed. *Lake Baikal: A Mirror in Time and Space for Understanding Global Change Processes.* Amsterdam, The Netherlands: Elsevier Science, 2000.

Moles, Sarah, et al. *Wetlands for Our Future.* Carlton, Australia: Australian Conservation Foundation, 2008.

Moss, Brian. *Ecology of Fresh Waters: Man and Medium.* Malden, MA: Blackwell Science, 2010.

Murray-Darling Basin Commission. *Rivers as Ecological Systems: The Murray-Darling Basin.* Collingwood, Australia: CSIRO, 2001.

Palaniappan, Meena. *Peak Water*. Oakland, CA: Pacific Institute, 2008.

Patten, Michael A., Guy McCaskie, and Philip Unitt. *Birds of the Salton Sea*. Berkeley: University of California Press, 2003.

Pearce, Fred. *When the Rivers Run Dry: Water—The Defining Crisis of the Twenty-First Century*. Boston: Beacon, 2006.

Priscoli, Jerome Delli. *Managing and Transforming Water Conflicts*. New York: Cambridge University Press, 2009.

The Redlands Institute. *The Salton Sea Atlas*. Redlands, CA: University of Redlands/ESRI Press, 2002.

Salina, Irena, ed. *Written in Water*. Washington, DC: National Geographic, 2010.

Seidenstat, Paul. *Reinventing Water and Wastewater Systems: Global Lessons in Improving Water Management*. New York: John Wiley and Sons, 2002.

Shiva, Vandana. *Water Wars: Privatization, Pollution, and Profit*. Cambridge, MA: South End, 2002.

Tahoe-Baikal Institute. *Baikal Reader*. South Lake Tahoe, CA: Tahoe-Baikal Institute, 2004.

Thompson, Peter. *Sacred Sea: A Journey to Lake Baikal*. New York: Oxford University Press, 2007.

Tompkins, Christopher R. *The Croton Dams and Aqueduct*. Charleston, SC: Acadia, 2000.

U.S. Environmental Protection Agency. *The National Water Quality Inventory*. Washington, DC: U.S. Environmental Protection Agency, 2007.

United Nations. *Atlas of International Freshwater Agreements*. Washington, DC: United Nations Environment Programme, 2003.

———. *Chile Water Resources*. Jeju, Republic of Korea: Final Report from the Eighth Special Session of the Global Ministerial Environment Forum: Environmental Dimension of Water, Sanitation, and Human Settlements, 2004.

———. *Fresh Water Under Threat, Vulnerability Assessment of Freshwater Resources to Environmental Change in Africa*. Washington, DC: United Nations Environment Programme, 2009.

———. *Lake Baikal Basin–Russian Federation*. Cambridge, UK: United Nations Protected Areas Program, 2002.

———. *Water: A Shared Responsibility*. Washington, DC: United Nations Environment Programme, 2006.

———. *World Water Development Report: Water for People, Water for Life*. Barcelona, Spain: Berghahn, 2003.

Venable, Sondra. *Protecting Lake Baikal*. Saarbrücken, Germany: VDM Verlag, 2008.

Vigil, Kenneth. *Clean Water: An Introduction to Water Quality and Pollution Control*. Corvallis: Oregon State University Press, 2003.

Ward, Andy D. *Environmental Hydrology*. Boca Raton, FL: Lewis, 2004.

Watts, Michael. *Curse of the Black Gold: 50 Years of Oil in the Niger Delta*. New York: Powerhouse, 2008.

Index

World Bank, The, 52, 55
World Health Organization,
    14–15
World Heritage Site, 64
World Resources Institute, 117,
    118
World Water Council (France),
    25, 115
World Water Day (2009), 115

World Water Forum, 115
World Wildlife Fund, 54–55

Xiaowan Dam (China), 112
Xiluodu Dam (China), 112

Yangzte River (China), 19, 27, *30*,
    111, 124
Yellow River (China), 19, 27, 120

Yurok, 113–14

Zambia, 22–23
Zinc, 14
Zipingpu Dam (China), 114
Zooplankton, 59–60